THE NAMES OF GOD

THE

NAMES

OF

GOD

ANN SPANGLER

BESTSELLING AUTHOR

ZONDERVAN®
.com

For information on Ann Spangler, visit www.annspangler.com.

If you would like to invite Ann to speak to your group, contact her at
admin@annspangler.com.

ZONDERVAN

The Names of God
Copyright © 2009 by Ann Spangler

Requests for information should be addressed to:
Zondervan, 3900 *Sparks Dr. SE, Grand Rapids, Michigan 49546*

ISBN 978-0-310-09667-2 (softcover)

ISBN 978-0-310-09669-6 (ebook)

Interior design: Michelle Espinoza

HB 04.25.2024

CONTENTS

PRONUNCIATION GUIDE

Ab, Abba	AB, AB-ba
Adonay	a-do-NAI
Aster Lampros Proinos	as-TAIR lam-PROS pro-i-NOS
Basileus Basileon	ba-si-LEUS ba-si-LE-own
Christos	KRIS-tos
Ebed	E-bed
Ego Eimi	e-GO ay-MEE
El Chay	EL CHAY
El Kanna	EL kan-NAH
Elohim	e-lo-HEEM
El Elyon	EL el-YOHN
El Olam	EL o-LAM
El Roi	EL raw-EE
El Shadday	EL shad-DAI
Esh Oklah	AISH o-KLAH
Ga'al	ga-AL
Hashem	ha-SHAME
Hiereus	hee-eh-REUS
Huios Dauid	hui-OS da-WEED
Huios tou Theou	hui-OS tou the-OU
Huios tou Anthropou	hui-OS tou an-THROW-pou
Iatros	ee-a-TROS
Iesous Soter	yay-SOUS so-TAIR
Immanu-el, Emmanouel	im-ma-nu-AIL, em-man-ou-AIL
Ish	EESH
Ish Makoboth	ISH ma-ko-BOTH

Kyrios	KU-ree-os
Leon ek tes Phyles Iouda	LE-own ek teys fu-LAYS YOU-dah
Logos	LO-gos
Lytron	lou-TRON
Machseh	mach-SEH
Magen	ma-GAIN
Maon	ma-OHN
Mashiach	ma-SHEE-ach
Melek	ME-lek
Metsuda	me-tsu-DAH
Migdal-Oz	mig-dal OHZ
Miqweh Yisrael	MIK-weh yis-ra-AIL
Nymphios	num-FEE-os
Pais	PICE
Pais tou Theou	PICE tou the-OU
Pater	pa-TAIR
Philos	FEE-los
To Phos tou Kosmou	to FOHS tou KOS-mou
Poimen Kalos	poi-MAIN ka-LOS
Prophetes	pro-PHAY-tays
Qedosh Yisrael	ke-DOSH yis-ra-AIL
Rhabbi, Rhabbouni	ra-BEE, ra-BOU-nee
Sar Shalom	SAR sha-LOME
Shophet	sho-PHAIT
Yahweh	yah-WEH
Yahweh Nissi	yah-WEH nis-SEE
Yahweh Roi	yah-WEH row-EE
Yahweh Rophe	yah-WEH row-FEH
Yahweh Shalom	yah-WEH sha-LOME
Yahweh Shammah	yah-WEH SHAM-mah
Yahweh Tsebaoth	yah-WEH tse-ba-OATH
Yahweh Tsidqenu	yah-WEH tsid-KAY-nu
Yahweh Tsuri	yah-WEH tsu-REE
Yahweh Yireh	yah-WEH yir-EH
Yeled	YEL-ed

INTRODUCTION

The Bible reveals many fascinating names and titles for God that can yield rich insights for Bible study. But these names and titles, particularly in the Old Testament, ...

added more questions to create the present volume. That allows readers to explore the richness of these names for themselves. Each of the fifty-two names and titles is presented in English (along with its rendering in Hebrew or Greek). Each section includes a key Scripture passage revealing the name, helpful background information, and Bible study questions designed for individuals and groups.

When studying the names of God, it helps to realize that names in the ancient world in which the Bible was written often functioned differently than they do today. In addition to distinguishing one person from another and linking people to their family heritage, names were thought to reveal the essential nature and character of a person. This is particularly true when it comes to the various names and titles of God revealed in Scripture. Furthermore, it was thought that to know God's name was to enjoy a kind of privileged access to him. Once his people knew his name, they could cry out to him, claiming his help and protection. But God's self-revelation also introduced a note of vulnerability. By associating his name so closely with a particular people, he risked the possibility that they would dishonor it by behaving in ways that contradicted his character.

The Names of God: 52 Bible Studies for Individuals and Groups rests on the premise that we can experience God in fresh ways by encountering his names and titles in the Scriptures and by learning about the biblical and cultural context in which these were revealed.

Names like *Abba,* "Father," *Yahweh Yireh,* "The Lord Will Provide," and *El Shadday,* "God Almighty," spread comfort, hope, and awe, while names like *Esh Oklah,* "Consuming Fire," and *El Kanna,* "Jealous God," challenge us to a purer, more passionate commitment. The same is true for the names and titles of Jesus, which yield a rich and deeper understanding of his character and purpose. *Yeshua,* the Hebrew equivalent of "Jesus," for instance, is linked to the most sacred name of God in the Old Testament. Titles like "Bright Morning Star" and "Prince of

Peace" are not only beautiful but deeply meaningful, revealing facets of Jesus' life and ministry we may have previously overlooked.

My hope is that all who undertake this study of the names and titles of God will be richly rewarded, recognizing many surprising connections between the Old and New Testaments, revealing a God whose forgiveness, love, and determination to help and to save is utterly consistent. My prayer is that everyone who encounters God's name within the Bible will be led into a deeper experience of his goodness and love.

Special thanks go to associate publisher and executive editor Sandy Vander Zicht, who offered many helpful suggestions regarding this manuscript, and to senior editor at large Verlyn Verbrugge, whose assistance with this and previous books has also been vital. Beth Feia crafted additional questions to those that originally appeared in *Praying the Names of God* and *Praying the Names of Jesus,* and I am grateful for her careful work on these. Thanks also to my assistant, Barbara Adams, who helped organize some of the material in the manuscript. Finally, I am grateful for the efforts of marketing director Michael Cook and his team to spread the word about this Bible study. Publishing is never a solo adventure, and I am grateful for the team of people at Zondervan who have helped make this book possible.

GOD, MIGHTY CREATOR

Elohim is the Hebrew word for God that appears in the very first sentence of the Bible. When we pray to *Elohim*, we remember that he is the one who began it all, creating the heavens and the earth and separating light from darkness, water from dry land, night from day. This ancient name for God contains the idea of God's creative power as well as his authority and sovereignty. Jesus used a form of the name in his agonized prayer from the cross. "About the ninth hour Jesus cried out in a loud voice, '*Eloi, Eloi, lama sabachthani?*' — which means, 'My God, my God, why have you forsaken me?'" (Matthew 27:46).

Key Scripture
In the beginning God created the heavens and the earth. (Genesis 1:1)

God Reveals His Name in Scripture

In the beginning when God created the heavens and the earth, the earth was a formless void and darkness covered the face of the deep, while a wind from God swept over the face of the waters. Then God said, "Let there be light." God called the light Day, and the darkness he called Night. And there was evening and there was morning, the first day.

And God said, "Let there be a dome in the midst of the waters, and let it separate the waters from the waters." God called the dome Sky.

And God said, "Let the waters under the sky be gathered together into one place, and let the dry land appear." God called the dry land Earth, and the waters that were gathered together he called Seas. Then God said, "Let the earth put forth vegetation: plants yielding seed, and fruit trees of every kind on earth that bear fruit with the seed in it."

And God said, "Let there be lights in the dome of the sky to separate the day from the night."

And God said, "Let the waters bring forth swarms of living creatures, and let birds fly above the earth across the dome of the sky."

And God said, "Let the earth bring forth living creatures of every kind: cattle and creeping things and wild animals of the earth of every kind."

Then God said, "Let us make humankind in our image, according to our likeness; and let them have dominion over the fish of the sea, and over the birds of the air, and over the cattle, and over all the wild animals of the earth, and over every creeping thing that creeps upon the earth."

So God created humankind in his image,
   in the image of God he created them;
   male and female he created them.

God blessed them, and God said to them, "Be fruitful and multiply, and fill the earth and subdue it; and have dominion over the fish of the sea and over the birds of the air and over every living thing that moves upon the earth." God saw everything that he had made, and indeed, it was very good. (Selected from Genesis 1)

Understanding the Name

Elohim (e-lo-HEEM) is the plural form of *El* or *Eloah,* one of the oldest designations for divinity in the world. The Hebrews borrowed the term *El* from the Canaanites. It can refer either to the true God or to pagan gods. Though *El* is used more than 200 times in the Hebrew Bible, *Elohim* is used more than 2,500 times. Its plural form is used not to indicate a belief in many gods but to emphasize the majesty of the one true God. He is the God of gods, the highest of all. Christians may also recognize in this plural form a hint of the Trinity.

Studying the Name

1. "Genesis" is a word that can mean "birth," "history of origin," or "genealogy." What can you observe about who God is from this passage about beginnings?

2. What can you observe about the world he has made?

3. God gave human beings dominion over the earth. How might you honor the Creator in your stewardship of the earth?

4. In what ways do you enjoy and benefit from creation every day?

5. Since God made us in his image, he has instilled in us creative power. What are your creative gifts?

6. God seems delighted by what he has made, proclaiming it good and even very good. How does God's assessment of creation shape your own attitude toward the world? Toward yourself?

Passages for Continued Study

Genesis 9:6, 12–17; 28:10–22; 35:1–8; Psalms 18:28; 102; Isaiah 40:28–29; 41:10

2

THE GOD WHO SEES ME

EL ROI

An Egyptian slave, Hagar encountered God in the desert and addressed him as *El Roi*, "the God who sees me." Notably, this is the only occurrence of *El Roi* in the Bible.

Hagar's God is the one who numbers the hairs on our heads and who knows our circumstances, past, present, and future. When you pray to *El Roi*, you are praying to the one who knows everything about you.

Key Scripture

She [Hagar] gave this name to the LORD who spoke to her:
"You are the God who sees me,"
for she said, "I have now seen the One who sees me."
That is why the well was called Beer Lahai Roi
["well of the Living One who sees me"].
(Genesis 16:13–14)

God Reveals His Name in Scripture

Now Sarai, Abram's wife, had borne him no children. But she had an Egyptian maidservant named Hagar; so she said to Abram, "The LORD has kept me from having children. Go, sleep with my maidservant; perhaps I can build a family through her."

and me."

"Your servant is in your hands," Abram said. "Do with her whatever you think best." Then Sarai mistreated Hagar; so she fled from her.

The angel of the LORD found Hagar near a spring in the desert; it was the spring that is beside the road to Shur. And he said, "Hagar, servant of Sarai, where have you come from, and where are you going?"

"I'm running away from my mistress Sarai," she answered.

Then the angel of the LORD told her, "Go back to your mistress and submit to her." The angel added, "I will so increase your descendants that they will be too numerous to count."

The angel of the LORD also said to her:

"You are now with child
 and you will have a son.
You shall name him Ishmael,
 for the LORD has heard of your misery.
He will be a wild donkey of a man;
 his hand will be against everyone
 and everyone's hand against him,
and he will live in hostility
 toward all his brothers."

She gave this name to the LORD who spoke to her: "You are the God who sees me," for she said, "I have now seen the One who sees me." That is why the well was called Beer Lahai Roi ["well of the Living One who sees me"]; it is still there, between Kadesh and Bered.

So Hagar bore Abram a son, and Abram gave the name Ishmael to the son she had borne. Abram was eighty-six years old when Hagar bore him Ishmael. (Genesis 16:1 – 16)

Understanding the Name

In the ancient world it was not uncommon for an infertile wife to arrange for a slave girl to sleep with her husband so that the family could have an heir. In fact, Ishmael, the son born to Abraham and Hagar, would have been considered Sarah's legal offspring. Hagar and Ishmael might have fared better had Hagar not forgotten her place the moment she learned of her pregnancy. Still, Sarah's treatment of her seems inexcusable and harsh.

In the midst of her difficulties, Hagar learned that *El Roi* (EL raw-EE) was watching over her and that he had a plan to bless her and her son. One of Abraham's grandsons, Esau, married Ishmael's daughter, and it was the Ishmaelite traders (also referred to as Midianite merchants in Genesis 37:26 – 28), themselves descended from an Egyptian slave, who transported his great-grandson Joseph into slavery in Egypt.

Studying the Name

1. Why do you think the angel of the Lord began his communication with Hagar by questioning her?

3. What gave Hagar the courage to go back to Sarah and face her again? How might Hagar's demeanor have changed after her encounter with the angel of the Lord?

4. What images come immediately to mind when you hear the name *El Roi*, "The God who sees me"?

5. Sarah tried to "force God's hand" in order to have a family. Describe a time when you thought God did not see your need and you were tempted to take matters into your own hands? What happened?

6.   How have you seen God's mercy emerge from your bungled attempts to be in charge?

7.   How have you experienced God's watchful care?

Passages for Continued Study

Genesis 21:1–21; Deuteronomy 12:28; 2 Chronicles 16:9; Psalms 33:13–22; 121:3, 5–8; Proverbs 15:3; Matthew 5:8; 6:3–4

3

GOD ALMIGHTY

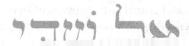

..., God Almighty, to Abram and told him of the everlasting covenant he was establishing with him and with his descendants. Until the time of Moses, when another divine name was revealed, the patriarchs considered *El Shadday* as the covenant name of God. When we pray to *El Shadday*, we invoke the name of the one for whom nothing is impossible.

Key Scripture

When Abram was ninety-nine years old, the LORD appeared to him and said, "I am God Almighty; walk before me and be blameless. I will confirm my covenant between me and you and will greatly increase your numbers." (Genesis 17:1–2)

God Reveals His Name in Scripture

When Abram was ninety-nine years old, the LORD appeared to him and said, "I am God Almighty; walk before me and be blameless. I will confirm my covenant between me and you and will greatly increase your numbers."

Abram fell facedown, and God said to him, "As for me, this is my covenant with you: You will be the father of many nations. No longer will you be called Abram; your name will be Abraham, for I have made you a father of many nations. I will make you very fruitful; I will make nations of you and kings will come from you. I will establish my covenant as an everlasting covenant between me and you and your descendants after you for the generations to come, to be your God and the God of your descendants after you. The whole land of Canaan, where you are now an alien, I will give as an everlasting possession to you and your descendants after you and I will be their God.". . .

God also said to Abraham, "As for Sarai your wife, you are no longer to call her Sarai; her name will be Sarah. I will bless her and will surely give you a son by her. I will bless her so that she will be the mother of nations; kings of peoples will come from her."

Abraham fell facedown; he laughed and said to himself, "Will a son be born to a man a hundred years old? Will Sarah bear a child at the age of ninety?" And Abraham said to God, "If only Ishmael might live under your blessing!" (Genesis 17:1 – 8, 15 – 18)

Understanding the Name

The Hebrew *El Shadday* (EL shad-DAI), often translated "God Almighty," may literally be translated "God, the Mountain One." Since many of the gods of the ancient Near East were associated with mountains, early translators may have made an educated guess regarding its meaning. Like the mountains themselves, God is seen as strong and unchanging. *El Shadday* reveals God not only as the one who creates and maintains the universe but who initiates and maintains a covenant with his people. *Shadday* occurs thirty-one times in the book of Job and seventeen times in the rest of the Bible. In the New Testament, the Greek term *Pantokrator* is often translated as "Almighty."

Studying the Name

1. Why do you think God revealed his name when speaking of the covenant he made with Abraham and his descendants?

3. What was Abraham's response to the revelation of God's name? How do you think you would have responded if God had revealed himself to you as he did to Abraham?

4. List the promises God made to Abraham. What was Abraham's response to this incredible news?

5. Have you ever had to wait a long time before God acted in your circumstances? Describe your experience and how it tested you.

6. What does the name *El Shadday*, God Almighty, mean to you? How have you experienced God's almighty power working on your behalf?

Passages for Continued Study

Genesis 12:2–3; 22:17; 49:22–26; 2 Samuel 5:9–10; Psalms 8; 91; Proverbs 18:10; Zechariah 1:2–3

4

THE EVERLASTING GOD
OR THE ETERNAL GOD

El Olam is the Hebrew name for the God who has no beginning and no end, the God for whom one day is like a thousand years and a thousand years are like one day. His plans stand firm forever, plans to give you a future full of hope. When you pray to the Everlasting God, you are praying to the God whose Son is called the Alpha and the Omega, the beginning and the end. He is the God whose love endures forever.

Key Scripture

After the treaty had been made at Beersheba, Abimelech and Phicol
the commander of his forces returned to the land of the Philistines.
Abraham planted a tamarisk tree in Beersheba, and there he
called upon the name of the LORD, the Eternal God. (Genesis 21:32–33)

God Reveals His Name in Scripture

At that time Abimelech and Phicol the commander of his forces said to Abraham, "God is with you in everything you do. Now swear to me here before God that you will not deal falsely with me or my children or my descendants. Show to me and the country where you are living as an alien the same kindness I have shown to you."

Abraham said, "I swear it."

Then Abraham complained to Abimelech about a well of water that Abimelech's servants had seized. But Abimelech said, "I don't know who has done this. You did not tell me, and I heard about it only today."

So Abraham brought sheep and cattle and gave them to Abimelech, and the two men made a treaty. Abraham set apart seven ewe lambs from the flock, and Abimelech asked Abraham, "What is the meaning of these seven ewe lambs you have set apart by themselves?"

He replied, "Accept these seven lambs from my hand as a witness that I dug this well."

So that place was called Beersheba, because the two men swore an oath there.

After the treaty had been made at Beersheba, Abimelech and Phicol the commander of his forces returned to the land of the Philistines. Abraham planted a tamarisk tree in Beersheba, and there he called upon the name of the LORD, the Eternal God. And Abraham stayed in the land of the Philistines for a long time. (Genesis 21:22–34)

Understanding the Name

Olam is a Hebrew word that occurs more than four hundred times in the Hebrew Scriptures. It is translated as "eternal," "everlasting," "forever," "lasting," "ever," or "ancient." It refers to the fullness of the experience of time or space. The title *El Olam* (EL o-LAM), meaning "Eternal God" or "Everlasting God," appears only four times. The word is applied to God and his laws, promises, covenant, and kingdom.

Studying the Name

1. Abimelech was the leader of the Philistines. What do his words say about the obvious nature of God's faithfulness to Abraham?

3. What images come to mind when you think of the "Eternal God" or the "Everlasting God"?

4. What might these names imply about the nature of God's promises?

Passages for Continued Study

Psalms 33:11; 90; 100; 103:13–18; 145:13–14; Ecclesiastes 3:11; Isaiah 40:28–31; 46:4; John 6:40; 17; Revelation 1:4–8

5

THE LORD WILL PROVIDE

YAHWEH YIREH

The Hebrew verb *ra'ah* (from which *yireh* is derived) means "to see." In this case, it is translated as "provide." Since God sees the future as well as the past and the present, he is able to anticipate and provide for what is needed. Interestingly the English word "provision" is made up of two Latin words that mean "to see beforehand." When you pray to *Yahweh Yireh*, you are praying to the God who sees the situation beforehand and is able to provide for your needs.

Key Scripture

Abraham looked up and there in a thicket he saw a ram caught by its horns.
He went over and took the ram and sacrificed it as a burnt offering
instead of his son. So Abraham called that place The LORD Will Provide.
And to this day it is said, "On the mountain of the LORD it will be provided."
(Genesis 22:13–14)

God Reveals His Name in Scripture

Some time later God tested Abraham. He said to him, "Abraham!"
"Here I am," he replied.

Then God said, "Take your son, your only son, Isaac, whom you love, and go to the region of Moriah. Sacrifice him there as a burnt offering on one of th

Abraham took the wood for the burnt offering and placed it on his son Isaac, and he himself carried the fire and the knife. As the two of them went on together, Isaac spoke up and said to his father Abraham, "Father?"

"Yes, my son?" Abraham replied.

"The fire and wood are here," Isaac said, "but where is the lamb for the burnt offering?"

Abraham answered, "God himself will provide the lamb for the burnt offering, my son." And the two of them went on together.

When they reached the place God had told him about, Abraham built an altar there and arranged the wood on it. He bound his son Isaac and laid him on the altar, on top of the wood. Then he reached out his hand and took the knife to slay his son. But the angel of the Lord called out to him from heaven, "Abraham! Abraham!"

"Here I am," he replied.

"Do not lay a hand on the boy," he said. "Do not do anything to him. Now I know that you fear God, because you have not withheld from me your son, your only son."

Abraham looked up and there in a thicket he saw a ram caught by its horns. He went over and took the ram and sacrificed it as a burnt offering instead of his son. So Abraham called that place The Lord Will Provide. And to this day it is said, "On the mountain of the Lord it will be provided." (Genesis 22:1 – 14)

Understanding the Name

Moriah, the site of Abraham's thwarted attempt to sacrifice his son, has been traditionally associated with the temple mount in Jerusalem.

Today Mount Moriah is occupied by a Muslim shrine called the Dome of the Rock. Jesus, whom John the Baptist called "the Lamb of God," is thought to have been crucified just a quarter mile away from Mount Moriah. It was there that *Yahweh Yireh* (yah-WEH yir-EH) provided the one sacrifice that would make our peace with him.

Studying the Name

1. Imagine that you are Abraham, making the three-day trip toward Moriah to sacrifice your son. What is in your heart?

3. Compare the scene in which a ram is sacrificed in Isaac's place in this passage to John 1:29: "The next day John [the Baptist] saw Jesus coming toward him and said, 'Look, the Lamb of God, who takes away the sin of the world!'"

4. Why do you think God tests people?

5. What is the most difficult sacrifice the Lord has asked you to make? How did you respond?

6. In what ways has God provided for you? Think about the last week, the last month, the last year.

Passages for Continued Study

Deuteronomy 15:4–5; Matthew 6:28–30; 1 Corinthians 10:12–13; 1 Timothy 6:17–19

6

LORD

יְהוָ֫ה

_____ Yahweh _____ occurs more than 6,800 times in the Old Testament. It appears in every book but Esther, Ecclesiastes, and the Song of Songs. As the sacred, personal name of Israel's God, it was eventually spoken aloud only by priests worshiping in the Jerusalem temple. After the destruction of the temple in AD 70, the name was not pronounced at all. *Adonay* was substituted for *Yahweh* whenever it appeared in the biblical text. Because of this, the correct pronunciation of this name was eventually lost. English editions of the Bible usually translate *Adonay* as "Lord" and *Yahweh* as "LORD." *Yahweh* is the name that is most closely linked to God's redeeming acts in the history of his chosen people. We know God because of what he has done. When you pray to *Yahweh,* remember that he is the same God who draws near to save you from the tyranny of sin just as he saved his people from tyrannical slavery in Egypt.

Key Scripture

God said to Moses, "I AM WHO I AM. This is what you are to say
to the Israelites: 'I AM has sent me to you.'"

God also said to Moses, "Say to the Israelites, 'The LORD [Yahweh],
the God of your fathers—the God of Abraham, the God of Isaac
and the God of Jacob—has sent me to you.'
This is my name forever, the name by which I am to be
remembered from generation to generation." (Exodus 3:14–15)

God Reveals His Name in Scripture

Now Moses was tending the flock of Jethro his father-in-law, the priest of Midian, and he led the flock to the far side of the desert and came to Horeb, the mountain of God. There the angel of the LORD appeared to him in flames of fire from within a bush. Moses saw that though the bush was on fire it did not burn up. So Moses thought, "I will go over and see this strange sight—why the bush does not burn up."...

Moses hid his face, because he was afraid to look at God.

The LORD said, "I have indeed seen the misery of my people in Egypt. I have heard them crying out because of their slave drivers, and I am concerned about their suffering. So I have come down to rescue them.... I am sending you to Pharaoh to bring my people the Israelites out of Egypt."

But Moses said to God, "Who am I, that I should go to Pharaoh and bring the Israelites out of Egypt?"

And God said, "I will be with you. And this will be the sign to you that it is I who have sent you: When you have brought the people out of Egypt, you will worship God on this mountain."

Moses said to God, "Suppose I go to the Israelites and say to them, 'The God of your fathers has sent me to you,' and they ask me, 'What is his name?' Then what shall I tell them?"

God said to Moses, "I AM WHO I AM. This is what you are to say to the Israelites: 'I AM has sent me to you.'"

God also said to Moses, "Say to the Israelites, 'The LORD, the God of your fathers—the God of Abraham, the God of Isaac and the God of Jacob—has sent me to you.' This is my name forever, the name by which I am to be remembered from generation to generation.

"Go, assemble the elders of Israel and say to them, 'The LORD, the God of your fathers—the God of Abraham, Isaac and Jacob—appeared to me and said: I have watched over you and have seen what has been done to you in Egypt. And I have promised to bring you up out of your misery in Egypt into the land of the Canaanites, Hittites, Amorites, Perizzites, Hivites and Jebusites—a land flowing with milk and honey.'

"The elders of Israel will listen to you. Then you and the elders are to go to the king of Egypt and say to him, 'The LORD, the God of the Hebrews, has met with us. Let us take a three-day journey into the desert to offer sacrifices to the LORD our God.' But I know that the king of Egypt will not let you go unless a mighty hand compels him. So I will stretch out my hand and strike the Egyptians with all the wonders that I will perform among them. After that, he will let you go." (Exodus 3:1–3, 6–8, 10–20)

Understanding the Name

Psalm 83:18; Isaiah 12:2; 26:4). This mispronunciation arose when in the tenth century Jewish scholars began supplying vowels to Hebrew words, which had formerly been written without them. Since *Adonay* was always substituted for *Yahweh* (pronounced yah-WEH, as scholars now think) in the biblical text, the Hebrew vowels for *Adonay* were inserted into the four letters of the Tetragrammaton: YaHoWaH.

Unfortunately, the translation "LORD," which is a title rather than a name, obscures the personal nature of this name for God. Though the meaning of *Yahweh* is disputed, the mysterious self-description in Exodus 3:14, "I AM WHO I AM," may convey the sense not only that God is self-existent but that he is always present with his people. *Yahweh* is not a God who is remote or aloof but one who is always near, intervening in history on behalf of his people. The knowledge of God's proper name implies a covenant relationship. God's covenant name is closely associated with his saving acts in Exodus. The name *Yahweh* evokes images of God's saving power in the lives of his people.

Studying the Name

1. Why do you think Moses asked God to reveal his name?

2. Make a list of everything God has revealed about himself in this passage.

3. What does this passage reveal about what was in the heart of God in regard to his people?

4. What was the catalyst for God's action?

5. Why do you think Moses was afraid to look at God?

6. Moses' reluctance is not hard to understand. Describe a time when you were similarly reluctant to do something you thought God was calling you to do.

7

LORD, MASTER

ADONAY

Adonay is a Hebrew word meaning "Lord," a name that implies relationship: God is Lord, and we are his servants. As a word referring to God it appears more than three hundred times in the Hebrew Scriptures. As you pray to *Adonay*, tell him you want to surrender every aspect of your life to him. Pray for the grace to become the kind of servant who is quick to do God's will. Remember, too, that the Lord is the only one who can empower you to fulfill his purpose for your life. In fact, it is in knowing him as your Lord that you will discover a true sense of purpose. The New Testament depicts Jesus as both Lord and Servant. In this latter role he exemplifies what our relationship to *Adonay* is to be.

Key Scripture
You are my Lord; I have no good besides You. (Psalm 16:2 NASB)

God Reveals His Name in Scripture

Moses answered, "What if they do not believe me or listen to me and say, 'The LORD [Yahweh] did not appear to you'?"

Then the LORD [Yahweh] said to him, "What is that in your hand?"

"A staff," he replied.

The L ORD [Yahweh] said, "Th..........................h."

...Moses said to the LORD [Yahweh], "O Lord [Adonay], I have never been eloquent, neither in the past nor since you have spoken to your servant. I am slow of speech and tongue."

The LORD [Yahweh] said to him, "Who gave man his mouth? Who makes him deaf or mute? Who gives him sight or makes him blind? Is it not I, the LORD [Yahweh]? Now go; I will help you speak and will teach you what to say."

But Moses said, "O Lord [Adonay], please send someone else to do it."

Then the LORD's [Yahweh's] anger burned against Moses and he said, "What about your brother, Aaron the Levite? I know he can speak well. He is already on his way to meet you, and his heart will be glad when he sees you. You shall speak to him and put words in his mouth; I will help both of you speak and will teach you what to do." (Exodus 4:1–5, 10–15)

Understanding the Name

Adon is a Hebrew word that means "lord" in the sense of an owner, master, or superior. It is frequently used as a term of respect and always refers to people. *Adonay* (a-do-NAI) is the plural form of *adon* and always refers to God as Lord or Master. In the Old Testament it is rendered as "Lord" (distinct from "LORD," the rendering for the Hebrew name *Yahweh*). When *Adonay* and *Yahweh* appear together, the NIV renders the name as "Sovereign LORD," while older translations of the Bible render it "LORD God." *Adonay* is first used in Genesis 15:2. In the New Testament, the Greek word most often translated "Lord" is *Kyrios*. (For more on Jesus as Lord, see chapter 41, p. 196.)

Studying the Name

1. How is the lordship of God displayed in Exodus 4? (Note that Pharaoh's headdress included a metal cobra, symbolizing his sovereignty.)

2. Imagine what Moses envisioned might happen to him if he obeyed the Lord? When might you have had similar fears about obeying the Lord?

3. Why was the Lord angry with Moses?

4. Notice that Moses expressed reluctance to doing God's will at the same time he was addressing him as "Lord." Have you ever done the same? What held you back from doing what the Lord was asking?

5. Although God was angry with Moses, how did he respond to Moses' request to send someone else?

6. Has God ever sent someone to come alongside you when you were insecure and hesitant about obeying God? Describe how this person helped you.

8

THE LORD WHO HEALS

YAHWEH ROPHE

The Hebrew word *rophe* means "heal," "cure," "restore," or "make whole." Shortly after his people left Egypt for the Promised Land, God revealed himself as *Yahweh Rophe,* "the LORD who heals." The Hebrew Scriptures indicate that God is the source of all healing. As you pray to *Yahweh Rophe,* ask him to search your heart. Take time to let him show you what it contains. If he uncovers any sin, ask for his forgiveness and then pray for healing. The New Testament reveals Jesus as the Great Physician, the healer of body and soul, whose miracles point to the kingdom of God.

Key Scripture

*If you diligently heed the voice of the LORD your God and do what is right
in His sight, give ear to His commandments and keep all His statutes,
I will put none of the diseases on you which I have brought on the Egyptians.
For I am the LORD who heals you. (Exodus 15:26 NKJV)*

God Reveals His Name in Scripture

Then Miriam the prophetess, the sister of Aaron, took the timbrel in her hand; and all the women went out after her with timbrels and with dances. And Miriam answered them:

"Sing to the LORD,

called Marah [meaning bitter]. And the people complained against Moses, saying, "What shall we drink?" So he cried out to the LORD and the LORD showed him a tree. When he cast it into the waters, the waters were made sweet.

There He made a statute and an ordinance for them, and there He tested them, and said, "If you diligently heed the voice of the LORD your God and do what is right in His sight, give ear to His commandments and keep all His statutes, I will put none of the diseases on you which I have brought on the Egyptians. For I am the LORD who heals you." (Exodus 15:20–27 NKJV)

Understanding the Name

The verb from which *Rophe* is derived occurs sixty-seven times in the Old Testament. Though it often refers to physical healing, it usually has a larger meaning as well, involving the entire person. Rather than merely healing the body, *Yahweh Rophe* (yah-WEH ro-FEH) heals the mind and soul as well. This Hebrew verb is also used in other ways—for example, God "heals" water, land, and nations, and he "repairs" an altar. Significantly, God also heals sin and apostasy. The Hebrew Scriptures, in fact, link sickness and sin by presenting sin as the cause of illness just as it is the cause of death. In the New Testament, the corresponding Greek word is *iaomai*, which can refer to deliverance from death, demons, sickness, and sin.

Jesus, the great healer, clearly indicated that sickness is not necessarily caused by sin on the part of the person who is ill. Rather, it can result from living in a sinful, fallen world.

Studying the Name

1. How did circumstances influence the people's attitude toward God? Describe times in your own life when your circumstances have caused your attitude toward God to fluctuate.

2. How did Moses react to the circumstances? What does his example teach about how we should respond to difficult circumstances?

3. The waters of Marah were bitter and God made them sweet. What areas of bitterness in your life might need to be healed or have been healed?

4. On what condition does God base his promise to keep the Israelites from disease?

5. Describe a time in your life when breaking God's commands caused you suffering or even sickness.

6. God tested the Israelites with adverse circumstances, thus uncovering what was in their hearts. Describe ways in which you have experienced God testing you. How did you respond?

8. How have you experienced God answering your own prayers for healing?

Passages for Continued Study

Psalms 38; 103:1–5; 147:1–6; Isaiah 53; 57:18–20; Jeremiah 17:14; Matthew 8:16–17; Luke 4:14–19; 8:50; John 9:1–7; James 5:14–15

9

THE LORD MY BANNER

YAHWEH NISSI

Ancient armies carried standards or banners that served as marks of identification and as symbols that embodied the ideals of a people. A banner, like a flag, was something that could be seen from afar, serving as a rallying point for troops before a battle. We know that banners were used in Egypt, Babylonia, Assyria, and Persia, and the Israelites apparently carried them on their march through the desert. When you pray to *Yahweh Nissi*, you are praying to the God who is powerful enough to overcome any foe.

Key Scripture
Moses built an altar and called it The LORD is my Banner.
He said, "For hands were lifted up to the throne of the LORD.
The LORD will be at war against the Amalekites from generation to generation."
(Exodus 17:15 – 16)

God Reveals His Name in Scripture

The Amalekites came and attacked the Israelites at Rephidim. Moses said to Joshua, "Choose some of our men and go out to fight the Amalekites. Tomorrow I will stand on top of the hill with the staff of God in my hands."

So Joshua fought the Amalekites as Moses had ordered, and Moses

Then the LORD said to Moses, "Write this on a scroll as something to be remembered and make sure that Joshua hears it, because I will completely blot out the memory of Amalek from under heaven."

Moses built an altar and called it The LORD is my Banner. He said, "For hands were lifted up to the throne of the LORD. The LORD will be at war against the Amalekites from generation to generation." (Exodus 17:8 – 16)

Understanding the Name

Unlike fabric flags, ancient banners were usually made out of wood or metal and shaped into various figures or emblems that could be fastened to a bare staff or a long pole. Depicting birds, animals, or gods, they often glistened brightly in the sun so that they could be seen from far off. A banner carried at the head of an army or planted on a high hill served as a rallying point for troops before battle or as an announcement of a victory already won.

Because banners embodied the ideals and aspirations of whoever carried them, they aroused devotion to a nation, a cause, or a leader. When Moses held up the staff of God in the battle with the Amalekites, he was holding it like a banner, appealing to God's power. By building an altar and naming it *Yahweh Nissi* (yah-WEH nis-SEE), "The LORD is my Banner," he created a memorial of God's protection and power during the Israelites' first battle after leaving Egypt.

Studying the Name

1. The Amalekites were fierce enemies of the Israelites and the first to attack them after their liberation from Egypt (see Deuteronomy 25:17 – 19). As members of God's people, we face spiritual enemies intent on destroying God's plans and purposes for our lives. What are some of the enemies you face and how have you dealt with them?

2. What does it mean to engage in spiritual battles today? What difference would it make if you could say, like Moses, "The LORD is my Banner"?

3. Aaron and Hur helped Moses when he grew weary of holding up his hands. Has God ever sent others to help you in the midst of battle? Who and how?

4. What battles might you be trying to fight in your own strength?

5.   How is Jesus God's banner of victory for us?

Passages for Continued Study
Numbers 21:4–9; Psalms 20; 60:4; Song of Songs 2:4; Isaiah 11:10–12; 49:22–25; John 3:14–15; 1 Corinthians 1:18; 15:52–57

10

CONSUMING FIRE, JEALOUS GOD

ESH OKLAH

EL KANNA

The Lord is a Consuming Fire who will ultimately destroy whatever is opposed to his holiness. He is also a Jealous God, who loves us completely and who, therefore, demands our wholehearted response. If we love him, we can be confident of his mercy, and our own zeal will make us jealous for God's honor and glory. When you pray these names of God, ask him to give you and the church a deeper understanding of his holiness and a greater desire to honor and exalt his name.

Key Scriptures

Do not worship any other god, for the LORD,
whose name is Jealous, is a jealous God. (Exodus 34:14)

Be careful not to forget the covenant of the LORD your God that he made
with you; do not make for yourselves an idol in the form of anything
the LORD your God has forbidden. For the LORD your God is a
consuming fire, a jealous God. (Deuteronomy 4:23–24)

God Reveals His Name in Scripture

Then the LORD said: "I am making a covenant with you. Before all your people I will do wonders never before done in any nation in all the world. The people you live among will see how awesome is the work that I, the LORD, will do for you. Obey what I command you today. I will drive out before you the Amorites, Canaanites, Hittites, Perizzites

is a consuming fire, a jealous God. (Deuteronomy 4:23–24)

Fear the LORD your God, serve him only and take your oaths in his name. Do not follow other gods, the gods of the peoples around you; for the LORD your God, who is among you, is a jealous God and his anger will burn against you, and he will destroy you from the face of the land. Do not test the LORD your God as you did at Massah. Be sure to keep the commands of the LORD your God and the stipulations and decrees he has given you. Do what is right and good in the LORD's sight, so that it may go well with you and you may go in and take over the good land that the LORD promised on oath to your forefathers, thrusting out all your enemies before you, as the LORD said. (Deuteronomy 6:13–19)

Understanding the Name

God sometimes manifested himself through images of fire—as a blazing torch, in the burning bush, or as a pillar of fire. When Moses met with God on Mount Sinai, the Israelites thought the glory of the Lord looked like a consuming fire on top of the mountain.

Most often, when Scripture pictures God as a consuming fire [*Esh Oklah*; AISH o-KLAH], it is in connection with expressions of divine anger against the sins of human beings and nations. Even so, his jealousy is not the "green-eyed monster" so often associated with human jealousy. As biblical scholar Edward Mac pointed out: "This word ... did not bear the evil meaning now associated with it in our usage, but rather signified 'righteous zeal,' Jehovah's zeal for His own name or glory."

Notes

Even so, Scripture compares God's jealousy to what a husband feels when his wife has been unfaithful. No wonder the first of the Ten Commandments prohibits the worship of other gods. The Lord is a Jealous God [*El Kanna*; EL kan-NAH], who cannot endure unfaithfulness. Jesus expressed this same kind of exclusiveness when he told his disciples: "I am the way and the truth and the life. No one comes to the Father except through me. If you really knew me, you would know my Father as well. From now on, you do know him and have seen him" (John 14:6–7).

Studying the Name

1. What promises does God make in the Exodus passage?

3. What warnings does he issue?

4. Why do you think the Lord said that his name is "Jealous"?

5. What is the significance of this particular title of God in relation to his covenant?

6. How does this name of God relate to your own life? To the church today?

Passages for Continued Study

Exodus 24:15; 34:14; Deuteronomy 4:23–24; 5:8–10; Psalm 18:6–17;
Song of Songs 8:6–7; Isaiah 33:14–15; 64:1–8; Daniel 3:1–25; Zechariah 2:5;
Malachi 3:2–3; Hebrews 12:28–29

11

HOLY ONE OF ISRAEL

The title "Holy One of Israel" emphasizes God's uniqueness, otherness, and mystery as well as his call to his people to become holy as he is. The Israelites were to be set apart for God, devoted to his service, and committed to honoring his character by reflecting it in all their relationships. In the New Testament Jesus was recognized as the Holy One of God by demons who were threatened by his power and purity. As believers, we are called to reflect the character of Christ, to be holy even as he is holy.

When you pray to the Holy One of Israel, you are praying to the God whose holiness not only encompasses his separation from evil, but his power, knowledge, justice, mercy, goodness, and love.

Key Scripture

The LORD said to Moses, "Speak to the entire assembly of Israel and say to them: 'Be holy because I, the LORD your God, am holy.'" (Leviticus 19:1–2)

God Reveals His Name in Scripture

The LORD said to Moses, "Speak to the entire assembly of Israel and say to them: 'Be holy because I, the LORD your God, am holy.

"'Each of you must respect his mother and father, and you must observe my Sabbaths. I am the LORD your God.

"'Do not turn to idols or make gods of cast metal for yourselves. I am the LORD your God....

"'When you reap the harvest of your land, do not reap to the very edges of your field or gather the gleanings of your harvest. Do not go over your vineyard a second time or pick up the grapes that have fallen. Leave them for the poor and the alien. I am the LORD your God.

"'Do not steal.

"'Do not lie.

"'Do not deceive one another.

"'Do not swear falsely by my name and so profane the name of your God. I am the LORD.

"'Do not defraud your neighbor or rob him.

"'Do not hold back the wages of a hired man overnight.

"'Do not curse the deaf or put a stumbling block in front of the blind, but fear your God. I am the LORD.

"'Do not pervert justice; do not show partiality to the poor or favoritism to the great, but judge your neighbor fairly.

"'Do not go about spreading slander among your people.

"'Do not do anything that endangers your neighbor's life. I am the LORD.

"'Do not hate your brother in your heart. Rebuke your neighbor frankly so you will not share in his guilt.

"'Do not seek revenge or bear a grudge against one of your people, but love your neighbor as yourself. I am the LORD.'" (Leviticus 19:1–4, 9–18)

Understanding the Name

Qedosh is Hebrew for "Holy One," a title for God that appears most frequently in the book of Isaiah, though it also appears in some of the other prophets (notably Hosea, Jeremiah, Ezekiel, and Habakkuk) and in Psalms and Job. It emphasizes God's otherness, separateness, and mystery. The term most frequently used for "holy" in the New Testament is *hagios*.

To understand the title "Holy One of Israel," *Qedosh Yisrael* (ke-DOSH yis-ra-AIL), we need first to understand that holiness is grounded in God's nature. It refers not to one of his attributes but to the totality of his perfection. In his holiness, God exists above and apart from the world he has made.

Things, times, places, people, and other created beings became

himself the perfect offering for our sins. Believers are called to be holy as he is holy and are enabled to imitate Christ by the grace of the Holy Spirit.

Studying the Name

1. In Leviticus 19, God links his commandments to his name. Why do you think he keeps reminding the people that he is "the LORD your God"?

2. If this were the only passage of Scripture you had ever read, what would it lead you to believe about God's character?

3. Notice that all the commands involve relationships. What kinds of relationships are highlighted in this passage?

4. Read through these commandments prayerfully, asking the Holy Spirit to show you where you need to make changes in order to live according to God's guidelines for holiness. What areas in your life are highlighted?

5. What relationships in your life need attention, repentance, or forgiveness?

6. How can you pursue being generous, loving, honest, truthful, and just toward those in your sphere of influence? Think of some specific examples.

12

THE LORD IS PEACE

YAHWEH SHALOM

Shalom is a Hebrew word, so much richer in its range of meanings than the English word "peace," which usually refers to the absence of outward conflict or to a state of inner calm. The concept of *shalom* includes these ideas but goes beyond them, meaning "wholeness," "completeness," "finished word," "perfection," "safety," or "wellness." *Shalom* comes from living in harmony with God. The fruit of that harmony is harmony with others, prosperity, health, satisfaction, soundness, wholeness, and well-being. When you pray to *Yahweh Shalom*, you are praying to the source of all peace. No wonder his Son is called the Prince of Peace.

Key Scripture
So Gideon built an altar to the LORD there and called it The LORD is Peace.
(Judges 6:24)

God Reveals His Name in Scripture

Again the Israelites did evil in the eyes of the LORD, and for seven years he gave them into the hands of the Midianites. Because the power of Midian was so oppressive, the Israelites prepared shelters for themselves in mountain clefts, caves and strongholds....

The angel of the LORD came and sat down under the oak in Ophrah that belonged to Joash ... where his son Gideon was threshing wheat in a winepress to keep it from the Midianites. When the angel of the LORD appeared to Gideon, he said, "The LORD is with you, mighty warrior."

"But sir," Gideon replied, "if the LORD is with us, why has all this happened to us? Where are all his wonders that our fathers told us about when they said, 'Did not the LORD bring us up out of Egypt?' But now the LORD has abandoned us and put us into the hand of Midian."

The LORD turned to him and said, "Go in the strength you have and save Israel out of Midian's hand. Am I not sending you?"

"But Lord," Gideon asked, "how can I save Israel? My clan is the weakest in Manasseh, and I am the least in my family."

The LORD answered, "I will be with you, and you will strike down all the Midianites together."

Gideon replied, "If now I have found favor in your eyes, give me a sign that it is really you talking to me...."

Gideon went in, prepared a young goat, and from an ephah of flour he made bread without yeast. Putting the meat in a basket and its broth in a pot, he brought them out and offered them to him under the oak.

The angel of God said to him, "Take the meat and the unleavened bread, place them on this rock, and pour out the broth." And Gideon did so. With the tip of the staff that was in his hand, the angel of the LORD touched the meat and the unleavened bread. Fire flared from the rock, consuming the meat and the bread. And the angel of the LORD disappeared. When Gideon realized that it was the angel of the LORD, he exclaimed, "Ah, Sovereign LORD! I have seen the angel of the LORD face to face!"

But the LORD said to him, "Peace! Do not be afraid. You are not going to die."

So Gideon built an altar to the LORD there and called it The LORD is Peace. (From Judges 6)

Notes

Understanding the Name

Yahweh Shalom (yah-WEH sha-LOME) is a title rather than a name of God. *Shalom* is a common term for greeting or farewell in modern Israel. When you say *shalom*, you are not simply saying "Hello," or "Have a Good Day." In its deepest meaning, it expresses the hope that the person you are greeting may be well in every sense of the word—fulfilled, satisfied, prosperous, healthy, and in harmony with themselves, others, and God. *Shalom* is a covenant word, an expression of God's faithful relationship with his people. (For more on this topic, see chapter 34 on the Prince of Peace, p. 163.)

Studying the Name

1. What does this passage reveal about the way God deals with his people's unfaithfulness?

2. Think about a time in your life when you felt harassed by circumstances. What caused your difficulties and how did you respond to them?

3. Why do you think the angel called Gideon a "mighty warrior"?

4. Why did Gideon believe he was ill-equipped to be a leader and a warrior?

5. What comes to mind when you hear the term *peace*?

6. What might be stealing your peace? Do you have habits of worry and anxiety? Have you become too busy to seek the Lord? Have you made compromises that have eroded your faith?

Passages for Continued Study

Numbers 6:22–27; Psalm 122; Proverbs 3:13, 17; Isaiah 26:3; 66:10–12;
Jeremiah 29:11–14; Lamentations 3:19–24; Galatians 5:22–23; Philippians 4:6–7;
Colossians 3:12–17

13

THE LORD OF HOSTS

YAHWEH TSEBAOTH

The Lord of Hosts is a title that emphasizes God's rule over every other power in the material and spiritual universe. When Scripture speaks of "the host of heaven," it is usually speaking of celestial bodies, though the phrase can also refer to angelic beings. The word "host" can also refer to human beings and to nature itself. When you pray to *Yahweh Tsebaoth,* you are praying to a God so magnificent that all creation serves his purposes.

Key Scripture
But David said to the Philistine, "You come to me with sword
and spear and javelin; but I come to you in the name of the LORD *of hosts,*
the God of the armies of Israel, whom you have defied.
This very day the LORD *will deliver you into my hand."*
(1 Samuel 17:45–46)

God Reveals His Name in Scripture

Saul clothed David with his armor; he put a bronze helmet on his head and clothed him with a coat of mail. David strapped Saul's sword over the armor, and he tried in vain to walk, for he was not used to them. Then David said to Saul, "I cannot walk with these; for I am not used to them." So David removed them. Then he took his staff in his hand, and chose five smooth stones from the wadi, and put them in his shepherd's bag, in the pouch; his sling was in his hand, and he drew near to the Philistine [Goliath].

The Philistine came on and drew near to David, with his shield bearer, in front of him. When the Philistine looked and saw David, he disdained him, for he was only a youth, ruddy and handsome in appearance. The Philistine said to David, "Am I a dog, that you come to me with sticks?" And the Philistine cursed David by his gods. The Philistine said to David, "Come to me, and I will give your flesh to the birds of the air and to the wild animals of the field." But David said to the Philistine, "You come to me with sword and spear and javelin; but I come to you in the name of the LORD of hosts, the God of the armies of Israel, whom you have defied. This very day the LORD will deliver you into my hand, and I will strike you down and cut off your head; and I will give the dead bodies of the Philistine army this very day to the birds of the air and to the wild animals of the earth, so that all the earth may know that there is a God in Israel, and that all this assembly may know that the LORD does not save by sword and spear; for the battle is the LORD's and he will give you into our hand." (1 Samuel 17:38–47)

Understanding the Name

Yahweh Tsebaoth (yah-WEH tse-ba-OATH) is a title of great power. It occurs more than 240 times in the Hebrew Scriptures, reminding us that all of creation, even in its fallen condition, is under God's rule and reign. At times Scripture speaks of the Lord of Hosts leading a great army. Cherubim and seraphim; sun and moon; stars and sky; rivers and mountains; hail and snow; men and women; animals, wild and tame — all these worship the Lord and are at times called to fight on his behalf. The NIV translates this title as "LORD Almighty."

Studying the Name

1. Why do you think the story emphasizes David's inability to do battle in the king's armor?

2. Contrast David's attitude toward the battle with Goliath's.

3. David is an excellent example of righteous zeal. Have you ever expressed righteous zeal or holy indignation? When?

4. What gave David such confidence?

5. Remember times in your own life when you felt embattled. How did you deal with your struggles?

6. What one thing could you do today that would help you face future battles with greater faith?

Passages for Continued Study

2 Kings 6:8–23; Psalms 46; 80:19; 84:12; 148; Isaiah 9:6–7; 14:24–27; Zechariah 1:3

14

THE LORD IS MY ROCK

YAHWEH TSURI

What better word than "rock" to represent God's permanence, protection, and enduring faithfulness? When you pray to the Lord your Rock, you are praying to the God who can always be counted on. His purposes and plans remain firm throughout history. The New Testament identifies Jesus as the spiritual rock that accompanied the Israelites during their long journey through the desert. He is also the stone the builders rejected but that has become the cornerstone of God's church.

Key Scripture

Praise be to the LORD my Rock,
who trains my hands for war
my fingers for battle. (Psalm 144:1)

Notes

God Reveals His Name in Scripture

Praise be to the LORD my Rock,
  who trains my hands for war
  my fingers for battle.
He is my loving God and my fortress
  my stronghold and my deliverer....
Reach down your hand from on high;
  deliver me and rescue me
from the mighty waters,
  from the hands of foreigners
whose mouths are full of lies,
  whose right hands are deceitful.
I will sing a new song to you, O God;
  on the ten-stringed lyre I will make music to you,
to the One who gives victory to kings,
  who delivers his servant David from the deadly sword.
(Psalm 144:1–2, 7–10)

Understanding the Name

Rocks provided shade, shelter, and safety in the wilderness and were used to construct altars, temples, houses, and city walls. Heaps of stones were also used to commemorate important events in Israel's history. God's commandments, given to Moses, were etched on stone so that all generations would learn his law. The word "rock" epitomizes his enduring faithfulness. The Hebrew noun *tsur* is often translated "rock" or "stone," while *petra* is the Greek word for rock. To worship *Yahweh Tsuri* (yah-WEH tsu-REE) is to echo Hannah's great prayer of praise: "There is no Rock like our God" (1 Samuel 2:2).

Studying the Name

1. David praised God for delivering him from his enemies. What kind of enemies do you face or have you faced in the past? How have you dealt with them?

2. David expressed his sense of vulnerability with vivid images. Describe a time in your life when you felt particularly vulnerable.

3. How has God heard your cries for help?

4. David describes God as a rock, fortress, stronghold, and deliverer. What do these descriptions reveal to you about *Yahweh Tsuri*?

5. Knowing that God is your rescuer and deliverer, how might this affect your temptation to defend yourself or retaliate against those who are against you?

6. How would your life be different if you experienced more deeply the truth that God is your Rock?

Passages for Continued Study

> Exodus 17:1–6; 1 Samuel 7:10–12; 2 Samuel 22:2–4; 24:1–13;
> Psalms 62:1–2; 95:1; 125:1–2; Isaiah 26:3–4; Matthew 7:24–27; 1 Corinthians 10:1–5;
> 1 Peter 2:4–8

15

THE LORD IS MY SHEPHERD

YAHWEH ROI

For at least part of their history, the Hebrews were a nomadic people, wandering from place to place and seeking pasture for their herds of sheep, goats, and cattle. To sustain their livelihood, it was vital for shepherds to keep their animals from straying, to protect them from thieves and wild animals, and to provide them with plentiful pastures. In the ancient Near East and in Israel itself, "shepherd" eventually became a metaphor for kings. The Hebrew Scriptures speak of God as the Shepherd of his people and apply this image to religious leaders as well.

The New Testament presents Jesus as the Good Shepherd, who protects the lives of his sheep by forfeiting his own life. When you pray to the Lord your Shepherd, you are praying to the One who watches over you day and night, feeding you and leading you safely on the path of righteousness.

Key Scripture
The LORD is my shepherd, I shall not be in want.
He makes me lie down in green pastures,
he leads me beside quiet waters,
he restores my soul.
He guides me in paths of righteousness
for his name's sake. (Psalm 23:1–3)

God Reveals His Name in Scripture

The LORD is my shepherd, I shall not be in want.
  He makes me lie down in green pastures,
he leads me beside quiet waters,
  he restores my soul.
He guides me in paths of righteousness
  for his name's sake.
Even though I walk
  through the valley of the shadow of death,
I will fear no evil,
  for you are with me;
your rod and your staff,
  they comfort me.
You prepare a table before me
  in the presence of my enemies.
You anoint my head with oil;
  my cup overflows.
Surely goodness and love will follow me
  all the days of my life,
and I will dwell in the house of the LORD
  forever. (Psalm 23)

Understanding the Name

Shepherding was one of the earliest human occupations. A family's wealth was measured by how many sheep, goats, cows, horses, camels, and/or asses a man owned. Abel, Abraham, Isaac, Jacob, Moses, and David were all shepherds. Before David fought Goliath, he told Saul: "Your servant has been keeping his father's sheep. When a lion or a bear came and carried off a sheep from the flock, I went after it, struck it and rescued the sheep from its mouth. When it turned on me, I seized it by its hair, struck it and killed it" (1 Samuel 17:34–35).

It was the shepherd's responsibility to count each animal in order to make sure none had gone astray. At night, sheep were kept in simple enclosures, in caves or within walls made from bushes. At times, the shepherd would sleep with his body lying across the gate to the enclosure in order to keep the sheep safe. Though Israel's religious leaders were also referred to as shepherds, they were often chided for their failure to watch over the flock of God. Both then and now *Yahweh Roi* (yah-WEH row-EE) is the one true Shepherd of his people. (See also chapter 49, p. 235, on Jesus as the Good Shepherd.)

Studying the Name

1. Read the first three sentences of this familiar psalm slowly, then close your eyes. Imagine that you are the sheep. What do you see? What do you feel?

2. What does it mean to "restore my soul"? Describe a time when you felt in need of such a restoration.

3. Read the fourth sentence slowly. Imagine again that you are the sheep. What do you see? What do you feel?

4. How has the Good Shepherd's rod and staff protected, guided, or corrected you? How have you found comfort in his rod and staff?

5. Why do you think the psalmist introduces the imagery of a table?

6. How would your experience of daily life change if you really believed that goodness and kindness would follow you all the days of your life?

Passages for Continued Study

Ezekiel 34; Isaiah 40:6 – 11; 53; John 10:7 – 10, 14 – 18; Revelation 7:15 – 17

16

THE NAME

HASHEM

Shem is the Hebrew word for "name" (the "*Ha*" before it is the definite article, "the"). The Bible speaks of Solomon's temple in Jerusalem as the place where God's name would dwell — the place where his people could pray and be heard. Jesus himself prayed that the Father would glorify his name through him. He also promised to do whatever we ask in his name. Philippians 2:9–10 affirms that God has exalted Jesus and given him "the name that is above every name."

Key Scripture
Hear the cry and the prayer that your servant is praying in your presence this day. May your eyes be open toward this temple night and day, this place of which you said, "My Name shall be there," so that you will hear the prayer your servant prays toward this place. (1 Kings 8:28–29)

God Reveals His Name in Scripture

Then Solomon stood before the altar of the LORD in front of the whole assembly of Israel, spread out his hands toward heaven and said … "Hear the cry and the prayer that your servant is praying in your presence this day. May your eyes be open toward this temple night and day, this place of which you said, 'My Name shall be there,' so that you will hear the prayer your servant prays toward this place. Hear the supplication of your servant and of your people Israel when they pray toward this place. Hear from heaven, your dwelling place, and when you hear, forgive....

"When the heavens are shut up and there is no rain because your people have sinned against you, and when they pray toward this place and confess your name and turn from their sin because you have afflicted them, then hear from heaven and forgive the sin of your servants, your people Israel. Teach them the right way to live, and send rain on the land you gave your people for an inheritance....

"As for the foreigner who does not belong to your people Israel but has come from a distant land because of your name—for men will hear of your great name and your mighty hand and your outstretched arm—when he comes and prays toward this temple, then hear from heaven, your dwelling place, and do whatever the foreigner asks of you, so that all the peoples of the earth may know your name and fear you, as do your own people Israel, and may know that this house I have built bears your Name...."

When Solomon had finished building the temple of the LORD and the royal palace, and had achieved all he had desired to do … the LORD said to him:

"I have heard the prayer and plea you have made before me; I have consecrated this temple, which you have built, by putting my Name there forever. My eyes and my heart will always be there." (From 1 Kings 8:22–9:3)

Understanding the Name

God's name is associated with his glory, power, holiness, protection, trust, and love. To call on his name is to call on his presence. To act in his name is to act with his authority. To fight in his name is to fight with his power. To pray to his name is to pray to him. In fact, the very first mention of prayer in the Bible appears in Genesis 4:26: "At that time people began to invoke the name of the LORD." Though we are to exalt God's name and proclaim it to the nations, it is also possible to dishonor it, which is the same as dishonoring him. God's name is his reputation.

Though God's name is holy and powerful, it cannot be invoked as a magic formula. Rather, his name becomes powerful whenever it is uttered by men and women who are exercising their faith in God.

Jesus taught his own disciples to pray by saying, "Our Father who art in heaven, *hallowed be thy name...*" (Matthew 6:9 KJV). In John's gospel, Jesus prays to his Father, saying, "I have manifested thy *name* to the men whom thou gavest me" and "I made known to them thy *name*, and I will make it known" (John 17:6, 26 KJV).

When we pray to *Hashem* (ha-SHAME), we are praying to the holy God who dwells in our midst, hearing and answering our prayers.

Studying the Name

1. What does it mean to confess God's name? What is the connection between repentance and answered prayer?

2. Why do you think Solomon prayed that God would hear the prayers of foreigners when they prayed toward the temple?

3. How can Solomon's great prayer at the dedication of the temple in Jerusalem inform your prayers today?

4. What does God mean when he says he will put his "Name" in the temple?

5. How have you experienced God's response to your own prayers?

6. You are the temple of the Holy Spirit (see 1 Corinthians 6:19). Because the Spirit of God dwells in you, you can call upon his name at any time and in every need. What needs would you like to bring to God right now?

17

KING

MELEK

The Israelites believed that *Yahweh* was *Melek,* or King—not just over Israel but over every nation on earth. They understood that the temple in Jerusalem was the earthly symbol of God's heavenly throne, and they expected a coming Messiah who would one day save his people from their enemies, establishing his rule over the whole world.

The New Testament presents Jesus as the King of kings (see p. 158), whose perfect obedience ushered in the kingdom of heaven. For the last two thousand years, God's kingdom has continued to spread through every nation, tribe, people, and language, as men and women accept Christ's rule. When you pray to *Yahweh Melek*, you are praying to the God who watches over the whole earth and who will one day come in glory to usher in an eternal kingdom of peace and righteousness.

Key Scripture

Endow the king with your justice, O God,
the royal son with your righteousness.
He will judge your people in righteousness,
your afflicted ones with justice.
The mountains will bring prosperity to the people,
the hills the fruit of righteousness. (Psalm 72:1–3)

God Reveals His Name in Scripture

Endow the king with your justice, O God,
    the royal son with your righteousness.
He will judge your people in righteousness,
    your afflicted ones with justice.
The mountains will bring prosperity to the people,

In his days the righteous will flourish;
    prosperity will abound till the moon is no more.
He will rule from sea to sea
    and from the River to the ends of the earth....
All kings will bow down to him
    and all nations will serve him.
For he will deliver the needy who cry out,
    the afflicted who have no one to help.
He will take pity on the weak and the needy
    and save the needy from death.
He will rescue them from oppression and violence,
    for precious is their blood in his sight.
Long may he live! (Psalm 72:1–8, 11–15a)

Understanding the Name

Compared to surrounding nations, the Israelites were relatively late in adopting monarchy as a form of government. Instead, they thought of *Yahweh* as their King. Once the monarchy was established, it was understood that the king received his power from God and was therefore responsible for ruling according to God's laws. David, Israel's second king, represented the ideal of how a king should rule.

But most of the kings of Israel and Judah fell far short of the ideal, leading people away from God by forging ill-fated alliances with foreign powers and by sanctioning the worship of false gods. After years of living under the rule of these less-than-perfect kings, God's people longed for a Messiah — a descendant of David who would sit on Israel's throne, subdue its enemies, and then rule over the entire earth. Given these expectations, it is hardly surprising that even Jesus' disciples thought he would establish an earthly kingdom.

Studying the Name

1. This psalm may have been a coronation prayer for one of the Davidic kings. Though it doesn't directly refer to God as the King, it does reflect the values of our heavenly King. Describe these.

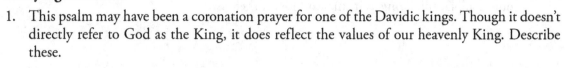

3. This psalm can also be read as a messianic psalm. How did Jesus fulfill this prayer?

4. How have you experienced Jesus' rule in your own life? What difference has it made?

5. Take a moment to list a few people and places in which oppression and violence reign. Pray for God's kingdom to come and his will to be done in troubled lives and desperate circumstances.

6. Do you eagerly anticipate the coming reign of the King of kings? In what ways might you have become complacent, living as if this world is all there is?

Passages for Continued Study

Psalms 24; 47:7; 97; Isaiah 9:6–7; 11:1–9; Zechariah 14:9; Matthew 13:24–30, 43; 25:34; Hebrews 4:16; Revelation 21:1–4; 22:1–5

18

HUSBAND

Hebrew Scriptures can also be translated "husband" (as well as "lord," "owner," or "master"), though this term usually refers to the Canaanite fertility god Baal (*ba'al* does occur in Hosea 2:16, "master"). Remarkably, in Isaiah and Jeremiah, this word is also used to describe God as the husband of his people, Israel. Though we never pray to *ba'al*, we do pray to the God who is the ideal husband, the one who provides for and protects his people and who refuses to divorce us no matter how unfaithful we may be. In the New Testament Jesus is presented as the bridegroom and the church as his bride.

Key Scripture

"In that day," declares the LORD,
> *"you will call me 'my husband';*
> *you will no longer call me 'my master.'...*
I will betroth you to me forever;
> *I will betroth you in righteousness and justice,*
> *in love and compassion.*
I will betroth you in faithfulness,
> *and you will acknowledge the LORD." (Hosea 2:16, 19–20)*

God Reveals His Name in Scripture

When the LORD began to speak through Hosea, the LORD said to him, "Go, take to yourself an adulterous wife and children of unfaithfulness, because the land is guilty of the vilest adultery in departing from the LORD." So he married Gomer....

She said, "I will go after my lovers,
  who give me my food and my water,
  my wool and my linen, my oil and my drink."
Therefore I will block her path with thorn bushes;
  I will wall her in so that she cannot find her way.
She will chase after her lovers but not catch them;
  she will look for them but not find them.
Then she will say,
  'I will go back to my husband as at first,
  for then I was better off than now.'...
"In that day," declares the LORD,
  "you will call me 'my husband';
  you will no longer call me 'my master.'...
I will betroth you to me forever;
  I will betroth you in righteousness and justice,
  in love and compassion.
I will betroth you in faithfulness,
  and you will acknowledge the LORD...."

The LORD said to me, "Go, show your love to your wife again, though she is loved by another and is an adulteress. Love her as the LORD loves the Israelites, though they turn to other gods." (From Hosea 1–3)

Understanding the Name

God's passionate love for Israel is reflected in the Hebrew word *Ish* (EESH), meaning "husband." When it is applied to God in the Hebrew Scriptures, it symbolizes the ideal relationship between God and Israel. God is the perfect husband—loving, forgiving, and faithful, providing for and protecting his people. This metaphor of monogamous marriage between God and his people is strengthened in the New Testament, which reveals Jesus as the loving, sacrificial bridegroom of the church. Our destiny, our greatest purpose as God's people, is to become his bride. (For Jesus as the Bridegroom and Husband, see chapter 45, p. 214.)

Studying the Name

1. Why would God tell Hosea to marry a woman who would break his heart and make a fool of him?

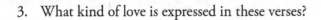

3. What kind of love is expressed in these verses?

4. What encouragement for your own life can you take from the story of Hosea and Gomer?

5. What encouragement can you take for the church?

6. Have you settled for a relationship that keeps God at arm's length? In what ways could you lower your guard and start responding to him, believing that he is your ideal husband?

Passages for Continued Study

Exodus 5:8 – 10; 20:4 – 6; 34:14; Song of Songs 8:6 – 7; Isaiah 54:5 – 8; 62:4 – 5; Jeremiah 3:14, 20; Ephesians 5:25 – 30

19

LIVING GOD

Maker of heaven and earth. He alone is the source of our life. We live because he lives. The prophet Jeremiah reminded God's people that "every goldsmith is shamed by his idols. His images are a fraud; they have no breath in them" (Jeremiah 10:14). This title sets Israel's God apart from the false gods of the surrounding nations.

Key Scripture

And Hezekiah prayed to the LORD: "O LORD, God of Israel, enthroned between the cherubim, you alone are God over all the kingdoms of the earth. You have made heaven and earth. Give ear, O LORD, and hear; open your eyes, O LORD, and see; listen to the words Sennacherib has sent to insult the living God." (2 Kings 19:15–16)

God Reveals His Name in Scriputre

Now Sennacherib received a report that Tirhakah, the Cushite king of Egypt, was marching out to fight against him. So he again sent messengers to Hezekiah with this word: "Say to Hezekiah king of Judah: Do not let the god you depend on deceive you when he says, 'Jerusalem will not be handed over to the king of Assyria.' Surely you have heard what the kings of Assyria have done to all the countries, destroying them completely. And will you be delivered? Did the gods of the nations that were destroyed by my forefathers deliver them: the gods of Gozan, Haran, Rezeph and the people of Eden who were in Tel Assar? Where is the king of Hamath, the king of Arpad, the king of the city of Sepharvaim, or of Hena or Ivvah?"

Hezekiah received the letter from the messengers and read it. Then he went up to the temple of the LORD and spread it out before the LORD. And Hezekiah prayed to the LORD: "O LORD, God of Israel, enthroned between the cherubim, you alone are God over all the kingdoms of the earth. You have made heaven and earth. Give ear, O LORD, and hear; open your eyes, O LORD, and see; listen to the words Sennacherib has sent to insult the living God.

"It is true, O LORD, that the Assyrian kings have laid waste these nations and their lands. They have thrown their gods into the fire and destroyed them, for they were not gods but only wood and stone, fashioned by men's hands. Now, O LORD our God, deliver us from his hand, so that all kingdoms on earth may know that you alone, O LORD, are God."...

That night the angel of the LORD went out and put to death a hundred and eighty-five thousand men in the Assyrian camp. When the people got up the next morning—there were all the dead bodies! So Sennacherib king of Assyria broke camp and withdrew. He returned to Nineveh and stayed there.

One day, while he was worshiping in the temple of his god Nisroch, his sons Adrammelech and Sharezer cut him down with the sword, and they escaped to the land of Ararat. And Esarhaddon his son succeeded him as king. (2 Kings 19:9–19, 35–37)

Understanding the Name

Scripture constantly warns against the worship of false gods. The first of the Ten Commandments is itself a proscription against idol worship. The title *El Chay* (EL CHAY), the living God, emphasizes God's role as Creator of all that is, in contrast with idols made of metal, wood, or stone, which are merely the creations of human hands. Jeremiah paints a vivid picture, saying, "The customs of the peoples are worthless; they cut a tree out of the forest, and a craftsman shapes it with his chisel. They adorn it with silver and gold; they fasten it with hammer and nails so it will not totter. Like a scarecrow in a melon patch, their

Notes

Studying the Name

1. Sennacherib ruled Assyria and Babylonia from 705–681 BC. He invaded Judah in 701 BC and threatened to attack Jerusalem when King Hezekiah refused to pay taxes. How does Hezekiah's prayer reflect his understanding of the "living God"?

2. Though Hezekiah asked God to deliver his people from their enemies, his prayer primarily focused on God's honor. How can his prayer be a model for ours?

3. How can this story of Hezekiah's reliance on the living God to defend his people be applied in the lives of God's people today? In your own life?

4. We too have enemies with which to contend, though often these enemies come from inside (like anger, addiction, depression) rather than outside. What difficulties besiege you or someone you love today?

5. What lies do you need to reject in order to trust in God's power to deliver?

6. Like Hezekiah did, what truths about God can you proclaim over these circumstances?

20

Dwelling Place, Refuge, Shield, Fortress, Strong Tower

MAON   MACHSEH   MAGEN

METSUDA   MIGDAL-OZ

These descriptive names for God often appear in clusters in the psalms as well as in other portions of the Scripture. When you pray to God your Refuge, Shield, Fortress, Dwelling Place, and Strong Tower, you are invoking the God who has promised to watch over you and keep you safe.

Key Scripture

He who dwells in the shelter of the Most High
will rest in the shadow of the Almighty.
I will say of the LORD, "He is my refuge and my fortress,
my God in whom I trust." (Psalm 91:1–2)

God Reveals His Name in Scripture

He who dwells in the shelter of the Most High
    will rest in the shadow of the Almighty.
I will say of the LORD, "He is my refuge and my fortress,
    my God, in whom I trust."
Surely he will save you from the fowler's snare

A thousand may fall at your side,
    ten thousand at your right hand,
    but it will not come near you.
You will only observe with your eyes
    and see the punishment of the wicked.
If you make the Most High your dwelling—
    even the LORD, who is my refuge—
then no harm will befall you,
    no disaster will come near your tent.
For he will command his angels concerning you
    to guard you in all your ways;
they will lift you up in their hands,
    so that you will not strike your foot against a stone.
You will tread upon the lion and the cobra;
    you will trample the great lion and the serpent.
"Because he loves me," says the LORD, "I will rescue him;
    I will protect him, for he acknowledges my name.
He will call upon me, and I will answer him;
    I will be with him in trouble,
    I will deliver him and honor him.
With long life will I satisfy him
    and show him my salvation." (Psalm 91:1–16)

Understanding the Name

The Hebrew Scriptures reveal a God who dwells with his people—first in a tent in the wilderness and then in the Jerusalem temple. The New Testament takes this idea of God's dwelling place on earth a giant step further by revealing a God who wants to dwell not merely *with* his people but *within* his people. Occasionally, Scripture reverses this imagery in a wonderful way by picturing God himself as our Dwelling Place or *Maon* (ma-OHN).

Closely allied to this image of Dwelling Place is the idea of God as our Refuge or *Machseh* (mach-SEH). He is pictured as one to whom we can run for safety and security. The word "refuge" also appears in the Hebrew Scriptures in connection to Israel's "cities of refuge" (the Hebrew word in this instance is *miqlat*), where people could flee for safety if they had accidentally killed someone. These cities were strategically located so that anyone in Israel was within a day's journey of one.

A shield or *Magen* (ma-GAIN) is another image of God's protecting care. Ancient shields were often made of layered cowhide and were used in situations of close combat as well as to protect soldiers from rocks hurled from city walls.

In biblical times, some cities were enclosed by walls, twenty-five feet high and fifteen to twenty-five feet thick. Farmers worked in the fields by day and then retreated within the city walls at night for protection. Large fortified cities also contained strongholds or strong towers that provided additional defense should the city's outer walls be breached. Like the other terms already mentioned, God is compared to a fortress or *Metsuda* (me-tsu-DAH) and to a strong tower or *Migdal-Oz* (mig-dal OHZ).

Studying the Name

1. What is characteristic of the person who experiences God as his or her refuge?

3. One of the more unusual metaphors for God in the Bible is that of an eagle or a great bird under whose wings the righteous can shelter. Compare this with Jesus' more domestic image of a mother hen who longs to gather her chicks under her wings (see Matthew 23:37). How would your life be different if you were able to take shelter under "the wings of God"?

4. What do you think it means to rest in God? How have you experienced this rest?

5. What dangers does the psalmist list in Psalm 91? What promises from God does he cite?

6.   What are the things you fear most? How can you apply God's promises to your fears?

Passages for Continued Study

Dwelling Place

Psalms 27:4 – 5; 31:20; 84; 90:1 – 2

Refuge

Deuteronomy 33:27; Psalms 9:9 – 10; 23; 46:1; 62:5 – 7; Proverbs 14:32; Nahum 1:7

Shield

Genesis 15:1; Deuteronomy 33:29; Psalms 3:2 – 3; 5:12; 28:7; 84:11; Ephesians 6:12 – 18

Fortress

2 Samuel 22:1 – 3; Psalms 46:2 – 7; 62:1 – 2

Strong Tower

Psalms 59:16 – 17; 61:1 – 3; Proverbs 18:10

21

JUDGE

character and nature of God. As Judge of the whole earth, he is the only one competent to measure the motivations of our hearts. In the Hebrew Scriptures, the word "judge" is often parallel to the word "king." When we pray to God our *Shophet* (sho-PHAIT), we are praying to the one whose righteousness demands perfect justice but who has also provided a way for us to be acquitted of our guilt through the life, death, and resurrection of his Son.

Key Scripture

Judgment will again be founded on righteousness,
and all the upright in heart will follow it. (Psalm 94:15)

God Reveals His Name in Scripture

Rise up, O Judge of the earth;
  pay back to the proud what they deserve.
How long will the wicked, O Lord,
  how long will the wicked be jubilant?
They pour out arrogant words;
  all the evildoers are full of boasting.
They crush your people, O Lord;
  they oppress your inheritance.
They slay the widow and the alien;
  they murder the fatherless.
They say, "The Lord does not see;
  the God of Jacob pays no heed."
Take heed, you senseless ones among the people;
  you fools, when will you become wise?
Does he who implanted the ear not hear?
  Does he who formed the eye not see?
Does he who disciplines nations not punish?
  Does he who teaches man lack knowledge?
The Lord knows the thoughts of man;
  he knows that they are futile.
Blessed is the man you discipline, O Lord,
  the man you teach from your law;
you grant him relief from days of trouble,
  till a pit is dug for the wicked.
For the Lord will not reject his people;
  he will never forsake his inheritance.
Judgment will again be founded on righteousness,
  and all the upright in heart will follow it. (Psalm 94:2 – 15)

Understanding the Name

The Hebrew verb *shapat* (sha-PHAT) can be translated in a variety of ways, including "judge," "govern," "vindicate," "decide," "defend," and "deliver." In the Hebrew Scriptures the word often combined the three primary functions of government — the executive, legislative, and judicial — that modern Western nations separate. That's why leaders like Gideon, Samson, and Deborah were called judges. When we read the Hebrew noun "judge" (*shophet*, sho-PHAIT) in the Hebrew Bible, we need to remember that it often connotes the broader meaning of "ruler."

The prophets often chided Israel's rulers for failing to act justly, reserving their harshest words for those who ignored the rights of aliens, the poor, the fatherless, and the widow.

When the word "judge" is used in the New Testament, it tends to

Studying the Name

1. Who are the victims of injustice whom the psalmist names? How are such people still victimized in the world today?

2. What reason does the psalmist give for the brazenness of those who do evil? How does their perception of God shape our own world?

3. Contrast the fool and the wise person as described by the psalmist.

4. How have you experienced God's discipline in your life? What has been the fruit of it?

5. Why do you think justice is often something we have to wait for?

6. Why do you think that people sometimes object to the idea of God as a judge?

Passages for Continued Study

Psalms 72:1–19; 94:1–15; 96:10–13; Isaiah 11:1–9; 30:18; Matthew 7:1–5; 25:34–36; John 5:24–27; Romans 2:1–4; Revelation 20:11–15

22

HOPE OF ISRAEL

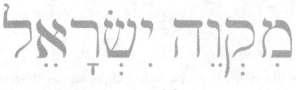

MIQWEH YISRAEL

Hope is the great stabilizer. It steadies us in times of fear and difficulty, not because we know that everything will turn out as we want, but because we know that God is trustworthy. Hope is what helps us stay on course regardless of circumstances. Biblical hope finds its roots in God and in his goodness, mercy, and power. We exercise our hope when we endure patiently. We nurture our hope when we read God's Word. Though we hope for earthly blessings, our greatest hope is aimed at the life to come, when God will not only wipe away our tears but invite us to share his joy forever. When you pray to *Miqweh Yisrael*, the Hope of Israel, you are praying to the one who saves all those who trust in him.

Key Scripture

Blessed are those who trust in the LORD,
whose trust is the LORD.
They shall be like a tree planted by water,
sending out its roots by the stream.
It shall not fear when heat comes,
and its leaves shall always stay green;
in the year of drought it is not anxious,
and does not cease to bear fruit....
O hope of Israel! O LORD! (Jeremiah 17:7–8, 13)

God Reveals His Name in Scripture

Thus says the LORD:
Cursed are those who trust in mere mortals
    and make mere flesh their strength,
      whose hearts turn away from the LORD.
They shall be like a shrub in the desert,

    and its leaves shall stay green;
in the year of drought it is not anxious
    and it does not cease to bear fruit....
O hope of Israel! O LORD!
    All who forsake you shall be put to shame;
those who turn away from you shall be recorded in the
        underworld,
    for they have forsaken the fountain of living water, the LORD.
      (Jeremiah 17:5–8, 13)

Understanding the Name

In the Hebrew Scriptures, hope is often connected to the expectation that God is a deliverer who will save those who trust in him. It urges us to wait confidently for him to act. In the New Testament hope is rooted firmly in Jesus — in his life, death, and resurrection as well as in his coming again in glory. We can also have hope for this life because the Holy Spirit indwells us, re-creating the image of Christ within us. Biblical hope is a new kind of strength, enabling us to be patient and enduring regardless of what we face. *Miqweh Yisrael* (MIK-weh yis-ra-AIL), the Hope of Israel — he is the God who saves his people.

Studying the Name

1. What does it mean to put your trust in people? Give some examples.

2. What does it mean to put your hope in the Lord? How have you been able to hope in him?

3. Where are you tempted to place your hope other than in God?

4. Describe what you are hoping for in your life. How do your hopes connect with the promise implied by this title of God?

5. Think of a situation in your life for which you need renewed hope. What habits of thought undercut your hope and breed unbelief?

Passages for Continued Study

Job 13:15; Psalms 25:2–5; 33:16–22; 46:2–3; 52:8–9; 119:81; 130:6–7; Isaiah 40:31; Jeremiah 14:8; Lamentations 3:21–23; John 16:20–22; Acts 2:26–28; Romans 5:1–5; 8:28–38; 1 Timothy 1:1; Titus 2:11–14; Hebrews 6:19; 1 Peter 1:3–6

23

THE LORD OUR RIGHTEOUSNESS

YAHWEH TSIDQENU

Righteousness isn't a popular word in our culture. Yet righteousness is essential to our happiness because it involves being in right relationship or right standing with God and conforming to his character, fulfilling our responsibilities toward him and others. But righteousness is impossible for us to achieve, no matter how much we long for it. It comes only as God's gift to us through faith in his Son. When we pray to the Lord Our Righteousness, we are praying to the one who has intervened on our behalf to restore us to his likeness and therefore to fellowship with himself.

Key Scripture

In his days Judah will be saved
and Israel will live in safety.
This is the name by which he will be called:
The LORD Our Righteousness. (Jeremiah 23:6)

God Reveals His Name in Scripture

"The days are coming," declares the LORD,
  "when I will raise up to David a righteous Branch,
a King who will reign wisely
  and do what is just and right in the land.
In his days Judah will be saved
  and Israel will live in safety

and they will be my people." (Jeremiah 23:5 – 6; 31:33)

But now a righteousness from God, apart from law, has been made known, to which the Law and the Prophets testify. This righteousness from God comes through faith in Jesus Christ to all who believe. There is no difference, for all have sinned and fall short of the glory of God, and are justified freely by his grace through the redemption that came by Christ Jesus. God presented him as a sacrifice of atonement, through faith in his blood. (Romans 3:21 – 25a)

Understanding the Name

The Hebrew word *tsedeq* is usually translated as "righteousness" but can also be translated as "righteous," "honest," "right," "accurate," "justice," "truth," or "integrity." Righteousness primarily involves being in right standing with God. As such it concerns fulfilling the demands of relationship with both God and others. Though people were often called righteous in the Hebrew Scriptures if they observed the Law, Jesus and the writers of the New Testament stress that righteousness is not merely a matter of outward behavior but a matter of the heart — of thoughts, motives, and desires. The goal is not merely to *do* what God says but to *become* like him. In the words of Addison Leitch, righteousness "is primarily and basically a relationship, never an attainment.... Christian righteousness ... is a direction, a loyalty, a commitment, a hope — and only someday an arrival."

Notes

The prophet Jeremiah predicted the coming of a King who would be called "The LORD Our Righteousness" (yah-WEH tsid-KAY-nu). Jesus fulfilled this prophecy by restoring our relationship with God through his life, death, and resurrection. Paul proclaims in his letter to the Romans, "But now a righteousness from God, apart from law, has been made known, to which the Law and the Prophets testify. This righteousness from God comes through faith in Jesus Christ to all who believe" (Romans 3:21–22).

Studying the Name

1. Jeremiah reveals that the coming King will be known as "The Lord Our Righteousness." What comes to mind when you hear the words "righteous" or "righteousness"?

3. How has Jesus' sacrifice affected your relationship with God?

4. What do you think Paul means when he uses the phrase "faith in his blood"?

5. In Romans 3:23 Paul writes, "There is no difference, for all have sinned." How does this phrase affect the way you look at yourself in relationship to others?

Passages for Continued Study

Genesis 15; Job 40; 42; Psalm 23:2–3; Proverbs 10:6–25; 11:8; 13:21; Ezekiel 36:26–28; Matthew 5:6; Romans 3:10–31; 1 Timothy 6:6–12; 1 Peter 2:24

24

GOD MOST HIGH

אֵל עֶלְיוֹן

emphasizes that God is the highest in every realm of life. In the New Testament, Jesus is known as the Son of the Most High while the Holy Spirit is the power of the Most High. All who belong to Christ are revealed as sons and daughters of the Most High by imitating the Father in heaven. When you praise the Most High, you are worshiping the One whose power, mercy, and sovereignty cannot be matched.

Key Scripture

When that period was over, I, Nebuchadnezzar,
lifted my eyes to heaven, and my reason returned to me.

I blessed the Most High,
and praised and honored the one who lives forever.
For his sovereignty is an everlasting sovereignty,
and his kingdom endures from generation to generation.
(Daniel 4:34)

God Reveals His Name in Scripture

Belteshazzar [Daniel] answered [King Nebuchadnezzar], "My lord, may the dream be for those who hate you, and its interpretation for your enemies!... This is the interpretation, O king, and it is a decree of the Most High that has come upon my lord the king: You shall be driven away from human society, and your dwelling shall be with the wild animals. You shall be made to eat grass like oxen, you shall be bathed with the dew of heaven, and seven times shall pass over you, until you have learned that the Most High has sovereignty over the kingdom of mortals, and gives it to whom he will. As it was commanded to leave the stump and roots of the tree, your kingdom shall be re-established for you from the time that you learn that Heaven is sovereign. Therefore, O king, may my counsel be acceptable to you: atone for your sins with righteousness, and your iniquities with mercy to the oppressed, so that your prosperity may be prolonged."

All this came upon King Nebuchadnezzar. At the end of twelve months he was walking on the roof of the royal palace of Babylon, and the king said, "Is this not magnificent Babylon, which I have built as a royal capital by my mighty power and for my glorious majesty?" While the words were still in the king's mouth, a voice came from heaven: "O King Nebuchadnezzar, to you it is declared: The kingdom has departed from you! You shall be driven away from human society, and your dwelling shall be with the animals of the field. You shall be made to eat grass like oxen, and seven times shall pass over you, until you have learned that the Most High has sovereignty over the kingdom of mortals and gives it to whom he will." Immediately the sentence was fulfilled against Nebuchadnezzar. He was driven away from human society, ate grass like oxen, and his body was bathed with the dew of heaven, until his hair grew as long as eagles' feathers and his nails became like birds' claws.

When that period was over, I, Nebuchadnezzar, lifted my eyes to heaven, and my reason returned to me.

I blessed the Most High,
   and praised and honored the one who lives forever.
For his sovereignty is an everlasting sovereignty,
   and his kingdom endures from generation to generation.
(Daniel 4:19, 24–34)

Understanding the Name

Elyon, the title given to the highest of the Canaanite gods, was appropriated by the Hebrews as a title for *Yahweh.* Emphasizing God's transcendence, the name *El Elyon* (EL el-YOHN) is first used in relation to Melchizedek, the king of Salem, who was also called "priest of God Most High" and who blessed Abraham in the name of "God

Studying the Name

1. What does the king's dream and Daniel's interpretation indicate about the source of Nebuchadnezzar's greatness and prosperity?

2. Nebuchadnezzar may have been stricken by a rare form of insanity in which a human being believes he is a particular kind of animal. Why do you think his boasting led to this kind of punishment?

3. What does Nebuchadnezzar's story reveal about the link between sanity and humility?

4. How have you been tempted to take credit for God's blessings? Think, for example, about any tendency to take credit for your career, the gifts God has given you, or even well-behaved children.

5. If the good things of this life are clouding your vision of who God is, identify what or who is "most high" in your life. Is it God or something else—a relationship, a job, plans for your children, a dream for your future?

6. What can you do to acknowledge God's greatness? Think of something specific you can do today.

25

THE LORD IS THERE

YAHWEH SHAMMAH

Strictly speaking, *Yahweh Shammah* is a name for a city rather than a title of God. But it is so closely associated with God's presence and power that it has often been equated with a name for God, at least in popular parlance. The name in the New Testament that is most closely associated with it is *Immanuel,* "God with us," a name that was given to Jesus. *Yahweh Shammah* (yah-WEH SHAM-mah), "The LORD is there," reminds us that we were created both to enjoy and to manifest God's presence.

Key Scripture

And the name of the city from that time on will be: THE LORD IS THERE.
(Ezekiel 48:35)

God Reveals His Name in Scripture

I will gather them from all around and bring them back into their own land. I will make them one nation in the land, on the mountains of Israel. There will be one king over all of them and they will never again be two nations or be divided into two kingdoms. They will no longer defile themselves with their idols and vile images or with any of their offenses, for I will save them from all their sinful backsliding, and I will cleanse them. They will be my people, and I will be their God.

My servant David will be king over them, and they will all have one shepherd. They will follow my laws and be careful to keep my decrees. They will live in the land I gave to my servant Jacob, the land where your ancestors lived. They and their children and their children's children will live there forever, and David my servant will be their prince forever. I will make a covenant of peace with them; it will be an everlasting covenant. I will establish them and increase their numbers, and I will put my sanctuary among them forever. My dwelling place will be with them; I will be their God, and they will be my people. Then the nations will know that I the LORD make Israel holy, when my sanctuary is among them forever.

And the name of the city from that time on will be:
THE LORD IS THERE. (Ezekiel 37:21–28; 48:35)

Understanding the Name

Genesis is the story of beginnings. For a short while, it portrays an easy intimacy between God and the man and woman he made. But as soon as sin enters the picture, that intimacy is destroyed. Sensing that sin has rendered them unfit for God's presence, Adam and Eve try to hide. But God finds them and casts them out of paradise, barring the way back.

Nevertheless, he doesn't entirely abandon sinful humanity. Instead God begins to reestablish his relationship with them. He starts by choosing a people for his own. Then he delivers his people from their slavery in Egypt, as Deuteronomy 4:37 says, "by his *Presence* and his great strength." God dwells with his people first in the form of a pillar of cloud and fire, then in the movable tabernacle in the wilderness, and later in the Jerusalem temple.

But still God's people sin. Tragically, the prophet Ezekiel witnesses the glory of God departing from the temple because of their continued unfaithfulness. God is no longer there. Despite God's absence, the book of Ezekiel ends on a note of tremendous hope, predicting a time of restoration, when "the name of the city from that time on will be: THE LORD IS THERE."

Studying the Name

1. British preacher Charles Spurgeon once said that "whenever it can be said of an assembly, 'The Lord is there,' *unity will be created and fostered.* Show me a church that quarrels, a church that is split up into cliques, a church that is divided with personal ambitions, contrary doctrines, and opposing schemes, and I am sure that the Lord is not there." How have you experienced unity as a mark of God's presence?

3. What is the connection between keeping God's laws and living in his presence?

4. How do you experience God's presence in your life? Think back over the last week or the last month in particular. How has God been present with you in your work, your family life, your friendships, your difficulties?

5. Spend a few minutes imagining even one day of your life without God in it. Make a list of all the blessings of his presence that would be withdrawn.

6. When Nebuchadnezzar lifted his eyes to heaven, his sanity returned. When have you lifted your eyes to the Most High and had your perspective restored?

Passages for Continued Study

Exodus 33:12 – 17; 2 Chronicles 6:41 – 42; 7:1 – 3; Psalms 132:13 – 16; 139; Isaiah 43:2; 63:9; Jeremiah 15:1; Zechariah 2:10 – 13; Matthew 1:23; 25:31 – 46; 1 Corinthians 3:16; Ephesians 2:19 – 22; Colossians 1:15; Hebrews 1:1 – 3

26

FATHER

אב   ἀββά

PATER

Though the Old Testament provides many rich names and titles for God, the New Testament reveals him most fully. Jesus, in fact, shocked and offended the religious leaders of his day by claiming that he had a Father/Son relationship with the God whose name they feared even to pronounce. Furthermore, by inviting his followers to call God "Father," he made this the primary name by which God is to be known to his followers. Because of Jesus, we can boldly pray the prayer he taught his disciples, "Our Father who art in heaven...."

Key Scripture

While he was still a long way off, his father saw him and was filled with compassion for him; he ran to his son, threw his arms around him and kissed him.
(Luke 15:20)

God Reveals His Name in Scripture

Now the tax collectors and "sinners" were all gathering around to hear him. But the Pharisees and the teachers of the law muttered, "This man welcomes sinners and eats with them.". . .

Jesus continued: "There was a man who had two sons. The younger one said to his father, 'Father, give me my share of the estate.' So he divided his property between them.

"Not long after that, the younger son got together all he had, set off for a distant country and there squandered his wealth in wild living. After he had spent everything, there was a severe famine in the whole country, and he began to be in need. So he went and hired himself out to a citizen of that country, who sent him to his fields to feed pigs. He longed to fill his stomach with the pods that the pigs were eating, but no one gave him anything.

"When he came to his senses, he said, 'How many of my father's hired men have food to spare, and here I am starving to death! I will set out and go back to my father and say to him: Father, I have sinned against heaven and against you. I am no longer worthy to be called your son; make me like one of your hired men.' So he got up and went to his father.

"But while he was still a long way off, his father saw him and was filled with compassion for him; he ran to his son, threw his arms around him and kissed him.

"The son said to him, 'Father, I have sinned against heaven and against you. I am no longer worthy to be called your son.'

"But the father said to his servants, 'Quick! Bring the best robe and put it on him. Put a ring on his finger and sandals on his feet. Bring the fattened calf and kill it. Let's have a feast and celebrate. For this son of mine was dead and is alive again; he was lost and is found.' So they began to celebrate.

"Meanwhile, the older son was in the field. When he came near the house, he heard music and dancing. So he called one of the servants and asked him what was going on. 'Your brother has come,' he replied, 'and your father has killed the fattened calf because he has him back safe and sound.'

"The older brother became angry and refused to go in. So his father went out and pleaded with him. But he answered his father, 'Look! All these years I've been slaving for you and never disobeyed your orders. Yet you never gave me even a young goat so I could celebrate with my friends. But when this son of yours who has squandered your property with prostitutes comes home, you kill the fattened calf for him!'

" 'My son,' the father said, 'you are always with me, and everything I have is yours. But we had to celebrate and be glad, because this brother of yours was dead and is alive again; he was lost and is found.' " (Luke 15:1 – 2, 11 – 32)

...viting his followers to call God "Father." Rather than depicting God as a typical Middle Eastern patriarch who wielded considerable power within the family, he depicted him primarily as a tender and compassionate Father, who extends grace to both the sinner and the self-righteous.

The most frequent term for "father" in the New Testament was the Greek word *pater*. The first recorded words of Jesus, spoken to his earthly parents, are these: "Didn't you know I had to be in my Father's house?" (Luke 2:49). In John's gospel, Jesus calls God his Father 156 times. The expression *"Abba, Pater"* (AB-ba pa-TAIR) is found three times in the New Testament, all in prayer. It is the form Jesus used in his anguished cry in Gethsemane: *"Abba,* Father, everything is possible for you. Take this cup from me. Yet not what I will, but what you will" (Mark 14:36).

Studying the Name

1. Who is Jesus speaking to when he tells the story of the wayward son? What might be a counterpart audience in our world?

2. How have you experienced the kind of grace this father extended to his son?

3. Why do you think the wayward son fails to offer to become one of his father's hired servants, as he had planned?

4. How is grace offered to both the lawbreaker and the lawkeeper in this story?

5. With whom do you most identify in this story? Why?

6. Jesus does not tell us how the older son responded to his father's explanation. Why do you think the story is left open-ended?

Passages for Continued Study

Deuteronomy 33:27; Psalms 68:5–6; 103:13–14; Hosea 11:1–2;
Matthew 5:43–48; 6:9–13, 28–32; Luke 12:32; John 10:27–30; 2 Corinthians 1:3; 6:8;
1 John 3:1–2

27

IMMANUEL

IMMANU-EL

'Εμμανουήλ

EMMANOUEL

The name "Immanuel" appears twice in the Hebrew Scriptures and once in the New Testament. One of the most comforting of all the names and titles of Jesus, it is literally translated "with us is God" or, as Matthew's Gospel puts it, "God with us." When our sins made it impossible for us to come to him, God took the outrageous step of coming to us, of making himself susceptible to sorrow, familiar with temptation, and vulnerable to sin's disruptive power, in order to cancel its claim. In Jesus we see how extreme God's love is. Remember this the next time you feel discouraged, abandoned, or too timid to undertake some new endeavor. For Jesus is still Immanuel—he is still "God with us."

Key Scripture
All this took place to fulfill what the Lord had said through the prophet:
"The virgin will be with child and will give birth to a son, and they will call him
Immanuel"—which means, "God with us." (Matthew 1:22–23)

Christ Reveals His Name in Scripture

This is how the birth of Jesus Christ came about: His mother Mary was pledged to be married to Joseph, but before they came together, she was found to be with child through the Holy Spirit. Because Joseph her husband was a righteous man and did not want to expose her to public disgrace, he had in mind to divorce her quietly.

But after he had considered this, an angel of the Lord appeared

(Matthew 1.18–25)

Understanding the Name

The name "Immanuel" (im-ma-nu-AIL) first appears in Isaiah 7:14 as part of a prophetic word that Isaiah spoke to King Ahaz of Judah (the southern kingdom) at a time when Aram and Israel (the northern kingdom) had formed a coalition against Assyria. The prophet Isaiah counseled Ahaz not to join in their uprising against Assyria, the region's greatest power, assuring him it would not succeed. At the same time, he urged Ahaz to trust in the Lord rather than to appeal to Assyria for help against Aram and Israel, who were threatening to invade Judah for not joining their uprising. Then the prophet invited Ahaz to ask the Lord for a sign to confirm the prophetic word, but the unfaithful king refused, having already decided to place his trust not in the Lord but in Assyria.

In response to Ahaz's refusal to trust God, Isaiah proclaimed: "Hear now, you house of David! Is it not enough to try the patience of human beings? Will you try the patience of my God also? Therefore the Lord himself will give you a sign: The virgin will be with child and give birth to a son, and will call him Immanuel."

Shortly after that Aram and Israel were soundly defeated, exactly as Isaiah had prophesied. Many years later the southern kingdom of Judah was destroyed by Babylon and its people taken captive.

Matthew's gospel recalls Isaiah's prophecy, applying it to the child who would soon be born to Mary, the virgin betrothed to Joseph. The sign given hundreds of years earlier to an apostate king was meant for all God's people. In fact, the Bible is nothing if not the story of God's persistent desire to dwell with his people. In Jesus, God would succeed in a unique way, becoming a man in order to save the world not from the outside, but from the inside. *Immanuel, God with us,* to rescue, redeem, and restore our relationship with him.

Studying the Name

1. What does this title of Jesus reveal about his nature?

3. When have you struggled to believe that God is truly with you?

4. Matthew begins and ends his gospel (see Matthew 28:20) with the promise that God is with us. How would your life be different if you began and ended each day with the firm belief that God is with you?

5. Jesus said, "Never will I leave you; never will I forsake you" (see Hebrews 13:5). How should this truth affect your perspective, especially in difficult times?

Passages for Continued Study

Genesis 28:15; Exodus 3:11 – 12; Joshua 1:5, 9; Psalm 139:7 – 10; Isaiah 8:10; 25:4; 42:2 – 3; Matthew 28:20; Luke 5:8; John 14:15 – 21; 15:9 – 12; 1 Corinthians 3:16; Hebrews 13:5 – 6

28

LIGHT OF THE WORLD

According to Jewish tradition, one of the names for the Messiah is "Light." How fitting, then, that Jesus is called the "light of the world." John's gospel portrays Jesus as the light that vanquishes the darkness brought on by sin—a darkness that ends in death. Christ has opened the eyes of a sin-darkened world to the truth of the gospel. We who believe in him have moved from darkness to light, from death to life. When we pray to Jesus as the Light of the world, let us remember that we are calling on the one who was so determined to draw us into his light that he spent nine months in the darkness of his mother's womb in order to become one of us. Let us ask Jesus, our Light, to make us shine with his reflected glory.

Key Scripture

I am the light of the world. Whoever follows me will never walk in darkness, but will have the light of life. (John 8:12)

Christ Reveals His Name in Scripture

Through him all things were made; without him nothing was made that has been made. In him was life, and that life was the light of all people. The light shines in the darkness, and the darkness has not overcome it.

There was a man sent from God whose name was John. He came as a witness to testify concerning that light, so that through him all might believe. He himself was not the light; he came only as a witness to the light.

The true light that gives light to everyone was coming into the world. (John 1:3–9)

When Jesus spoke again to the people, he said, "I am the light of the world. Whoever follows me will never walk in darkness, but will have the light of life." (John 8:12)

Understanding the Name

The Hebrew Scriptures are full of images that link God with light — pillars of fire, burning lamps, consuming fire. Such images are often associated with God's nearness or his presence. John's gospel portrays Jesus as the embodiment of the divine light, a light so powerful that it cannot be overcome by the darkness of sin and death. Though Satan tries to disguise himself as an angel of light, he is light's opposite — the prince of darkness.

The phrase "the light of the world" — *to phos tou kosmou* (to FOHS tou KOS-mou) — appears three times in the New Testament (Matthew 5:14; John 8:12; 9:5). It is a distinctive phrase spoken only by Jesus, who uses it twice to refer to himself and once to refer to his disciples, who are to reflect his light through their good deeds.

Just as natural light is essential to life on earth, Christ's light is essential to unending life with God. Whoever believes in his light becomes like him, reflecting his brightness by walking in his light and obeying his commands.

Studying the Name

1. What do the terms "light" and "dark" mean to you?

3. Have you ever lived through a time of darkness? Describe what it felt like.

4. Have you experienced Jesus as light? If so, how?

5. In Matthew 5:14 Jesus said, "You are the light of the world." In what ways have you been or can you be a "light-bearer" in places of darkness around you?

6. First John 1:6 says, "God is light; in him there is no darkness at all." What does this mean to you?

Passages for Continued Study

Exodus 34:29 – 35; Psalm 27:1; Isaiah 9:2; 60:2, 19 – 20; Matthew 5:14 – 16; 17:1 – 2; Luke 2:29 – 32; John 8:12; Acts 9:1 – 22; Romans 13:12; 2 Corinthians 4:3 – 6; Ephesians 5:8 – 10; Philippians 2:14 – 16; 1 Peter 2:9 – 10; 1 John 1:5 – 7; Revelation 2:1 – 7; 21:22 – 27

29

CHILD

PAIS

A child was always at the heart of the biblical covenant. Already in the garden of Eden God promised that Eve's offspring would crush the head of the serpent who beguiled her. Later God made a covenant with Abraham, promising that Sarah would bear him a child who would be the first of countless descendents. Then Isaiah spoke of a child who would be born of a virgin and be given the name "Wonderful Counselor, Mighty God, Everlasting Father, Prince of Peace." The New Testament tells of the fulfillment of that promise, and Jesus presents children as the model for his followers to emulate. The only way to enter the kingdom is with the humility and trust of little children.

Key Scripture

Joseph also went up from the town of Nazareth in Galilee to Judea,
to Bethlehem the town of David, because he belonged to the house and line of
David. He went there to register with Mary, who was pledged to be married to him
and was expecting a child. While they were there, the time came for the baby to
be born, and she gave birth to her firstborn, a son. She wrapped him in cloths and
placed him in a manger, because there was no room for them in the inn.

(Luke 2:4 – 7)

Christ Reveals His Name in Scripture

In those days Caesar Augustus issued a decree that a census should be taken of the entire Roman world. (This was the first census that took place while Quirinius was governor of Syria.) And everyone went to his own town to register.

So Joseph also went up from the town of Nazareth in Galilee to Judea, to Bethlehem the town of David, because he belonged to the house and line of David. He went there to register with Mary, who was pledged to be married to him and was expecting a child. While they were there, the time came for the baby to be born, and she gave birth to her firstborn, a son. She wrapped him in cloths and placed him in a manger, because there was no room for them in the inn.

And there were shepherds living out in the fields nearby, keeping watch over their flocks at night. An angel of the Lord appeared to them, and the glory of the Lord shone around them, and they were terrified. But the angel said to them, "Do not be afraid. I bring you good news of great joy that will be for all the people. Today in the town of David a Savior has been born to you; he is Christ the Lord. This will be a sign to you: You will find a baby wrapped in cloths and lying in a manger." (Luke 2:1–12)

Understanding the Name

Though the Israelites considered children a great blessing, they occupied the bottom rung of the social ladder. Entrusted with the solemn responsibility of teaching and disciplining them, parents were accorded nearly absolute authority. To be a child was to be powerless, dependent, subservient. Yet even little children and young infants could receive wisdom from God and their lips could praise him. The prophet Isaiah spoke of a child, or *yeled* (YEL-ed), who would one day be born of a virgin and sit on David's throne. Luke's gospel tells us that Mary, while she was yet betrothed, was expecting a child, or *pais* (PICE), and that she gave birth to him in Bethlehem.

Studying the Name

1.   What images come to mind when you think of the child Jesus?

3.   Why do you think God allowed his Son to be born in such humble circumstances and to be placed in a manger?

4.   The Savior of the world, heralded by angels, came as a helpless, dependent, vulnerable child. Why do you think God chose this means of bringing us our Savior?

5.   If Christ made himself vulnerable in order to win the world, what implications does this have for the way you live as his follower?

6. Why might God's plan offend some people or seem like "foolishness"? What obstacles did this plan pose for many who encountered Jesus? For those who encounter him today?

7. What elements of the gospel still strike you as "foolish," things that are easier to read about than put into practice?

8. Jesus said to his disciples, "Unless you change and become like little children, you will never enter the kingdom of heaven. Therefore, whoever humbles himself like this child is greatest in the kingdom of heaven" (see Matthew 18:3–4). What does this admonition to become like a little child mean for your own life?

Passages for Continued Study

Genesis 3:14–15; Isaiah 7:14; 9:6–7; Matthew 2:13–20; 18:2–4;
Luke 1:26–45; 2:1–20; 9:48; 1 Corinthians 1:18–31

30

BREAD OF LIFE

ἄρτος ζωῆς

seems entirely reasonable for Jesus, in what has become known as the Lord's Prayer, to instruct his disciples to pray for their daily bread. Yet the Lord also challenged his followers not to work for food that spoils, announcing himself as the only food that would enable them to live forever.

In fact, Jesus was born in Bethlehem, which means "house of bread." After feeding five thousand people with only five loaves of bread and two fish, he shocked his listeners by declaring: "Unless you eat the flesh of the Son of Man and drink his blood, you have no life in you" (John 6:53). This week, as you seek to understand what it means that Jesus is the Bread of Life, ask him to show you exactly what it means to feed on him.

Key Scripture

I am the bread of life. Your ancestors ate the manna in the wilderness, yet they died. But here is the bread that comes down from heaven, which people may eat and not die. I am the living bread that came down from heaven. Whoever eats of this bread will live forever. This bread is my flesh, which I will give for the life of the world. (John 6:48–51)

Christ Reveals His Name in Scripture

When they [Jesus' followers] found him on the other side of the lake, they asked him, "Rabbi, when did you get here?"

Jesus answered, "Very truly I tell you, you are looking for me, not because you saw the signs I performed but because you ate the loaves and had your fill. Do not work for food that spoils, but for food that endures to eternal life, which the Son of Man will give you. On him God the Father has placed his seal of approval. . . .

"I am the bread of life. Your ancestors ate the manna in the wilderness, yet they died. But here is the bread that comes down from heaven, which people may eat and not die. I am the living bread that came down from heaven. Whoever eats of this bread will live forever. This bread is my flesh, which I will give for the life of the world."

Then the Jews began to argue sharply among themselves, "How can this man give us his flesh to eat?"

Jesus said to them, "Very truly I tell you, unless you eat the flesh of the Son of Man and drink his blood, you have no life in you. Whoever eats my flesh and drinks my blood has eternal life, and I will raise them up at the last day. For my flesh is real food and my blood is real drink. Whoever eats my flesh and drinks my blood remains in me, and I in them. Just as the living Father sent me and I live because of the Father, so the one who feeds on me will live because of me. This is the bread that came down from heaven. Your ancestors ate manna and died, but whoever feeds on this bread will live forever." (John 6:25–27, 48–58)

Understanding the Name

Bread was baked daily in the ancient world. Made from a variety of grains (barley for the poor and wheat for those with money), it was usually shaped into small round loaves that looked more like rolls or buns than the large loaves of bread we eat today.

Because bread was a primary staple, it was also used in various aspects of worship. Cereal offerings took the form of loaves or cakes, and bread was also used as a firstfruit offering or as a peace offering. The Bread of the Presence, consisting of twelve loaves of unleavened bread, symbolized the covenant between God and his people. Displayed in the temple sanctuary next to the Most Holy Place, it served as a constant reminder to the priests and the people that it was God who sustained the twelve tribes of Israel in the desert. Psalm 78:24–25 speaks of how God's people were fed in the wilderness:

> He [God] rained down manna for the people to eat,
>   he gave them the grain of heaven.
> Human beings ate the bread of angels;
>   he sent them all the food they could eat.

the Bread of Life.

Studying the Name

1. We live in an affluent, consumer-driven society in which "cheap bread" is sold on every corner. Give some examples of the food that fails to nourish.

2. Jesus knew that bread is one of life's necessities, yet he counseled his followers not to work for food that spoils. What are the implications for your life?

3. What do you hunger and thirst for that does not bring life to you?

4. Various Christian denominations have interpreted Jesus' words about eating his flesh and drinking his blood differently. How have these words impacted your own spiritual journey?

5. Discuss the various ways in which it is possible for you to "feed on Jesus."

Passages for Continued Study

Psalm 103; Isaiah 55:1 – 2; Luke 22:7 – 22; 24:13 – 35; John 6; Revelation 2:17

31

PHYSICIAN

ἰατρός

IATROS

Jesus, the greatest of all physicians, performed more healings than any other kind of miracle. Nothing stumped him—not blindness, craziness, lameness, deafness, or even death. Every ailment yielded to his undeniable power, and every healing served as evidence that his kingdom was breaking into our fallen world. When you pray for healing for yourself or others, remember that God never sends sickness, though he sometimes allows us to become sick. Indeed, Scripture sees sickness and death as by-products of sin. And it was to solve the sin problem that Jesus came into the world. When you pray for healing, remember that Jesus is always your ally, always wanting what is best for you and for those you care about.

Key Scriptures

The blind receive sight, the lame walk, those who have leprosy are cured, the deaf hear, the dead are raised, and the good news is preached to the poor.
(Matthew 11:5)

Jesus said to them, "Surely you will quote this proverb to me: 'Physician, heal yourself! Do here in your hometown what we have heard that you did in Capernaum.'" (Luke 4:23)

Christt Reveals His Name in Scripture

When John heard in prison what Christ was doing, he sent his disciples to ask him, "Are you the one who was to come, or should we expect someone else?"

Jesus replied, "Go back and report to John what you hear and see: The blind receive sight, the lame walk, those who have leprosy are cured, the deaf hear, the dead are raised, and the good news is preached

to preach good news to the poor.
He has sent me to proclaim freedom for the prisoners
    and recovery of sight for the blind,
to release the oppressed,
    to proclaim the year of the Lord's favor."

Then he rolled up the scroll, gave it back to the attendant and sat down....

Jesus said to them, "Surely you will quote this proverb to me: 'Physician, heal yourself! Do here in your hometown what we have heard that you did in Capernaum.'"

"I tell you the truth," he continued, "no prophet is accepted in his hometown." (Luke 4:16–24)

Understanding the Name

The ancient Egyptians were among the first to practice medicine, learning how to fill teeth, stitch up wounds, set broken bones, and perform various kinds of surgery. Later on the Greeks developed a more empirical approach to medicine, while the Romans grew wealthy by developing specialties that focused on treating eyes, ears, teeth, and various gynecological disorders.

Though the Jews used physicians, they believed healing came ultimately from God. He was *Yahweh Rophe*, "the LORD Who Heals" (see chapter 8, p. 42). What's more, their Divine Healer had given them a set of laws that included hygienic practices that contributed to their health and to their staying power as a people. Also, according to the Talmud, an authoritative collection of Jewish writings, every city had its own doctor who was licensed by city officials. The temple in Jerusalem also had its own physician, assigned to take care of the priests.

Jesus' healing miracles clearly reveal him as the greatest of all physicians. While he emphasized the importance of faith in the healing process, the Gospels do not support the teaching that a lack of healing always indicates a lack of faith. And though the New Testament sometimes directly links individual sin with sickness, it does not presume that every sickness is caused by individual sin. Rather, human beings become ill as the result of living in a fallen world.

It is interesting to note that the author of Luke's gospel, which recounts many of Jesus' healing miracles, was himself a physician (see Colossians 4:14).

Studying the Name

1. Why do you think Jesus responded to John the Baptist in the way he did in Matthew 11:2–5? What does this say about his purpose for coming into the world?

3. Do you think Jesus still heals people today? Why or why not?

4. Are there areas of your life that need the work of the great Physician?

5. Sometimes we have difficulty believing in God's healing power. If you struggle with this, describe what hinders you from trusting him to heal.

6. Have you experienced God's healing power in your own life? If so, how?

Passages for Continued Study

Jeremiah 33:6–9; Malachi 4:2; Matthew 8:5–10; 9; 11:2–5; Mark 9:17–29;
Luke 4:16–24; 8:43–48; 17:11–17; John 4:46–54; 2 Corinthians 7:13–14; 12:7–10;
James 5:14–16

32

LAMB, LAMB OF GOD

ἀμνὸν

AMNOS TOU THEOU

Most of us picture lambs as downy white animals frolicking in rolling green meadows or carried tenderly in the arms of their shepherd. Lambs represent gentleness, purity, and innocence. Though it is one of the most tender images of Christ in the New Testament, the phrase "Lamb of God" would have conjured far more disturbing pictures to those who heard John the Baptist hail Jesus with these words. Hadn't many of them, at one time or another, carried one of their own lambs to the altar to be slaughtered as a sacrifice for their sins, a lamb that they had fed and bathed, the best animal in their small flock? Hadn't the bloody sacrifice of an innocent animal provided a vivid image of the consequences of transgressing the Mosaic law? Surely, John must have shocked his listeners by applying the phrase "Lamb of God" to a living man. When we pray to Jesus as the Lamb of God, we are praying to the One who voluntarily laid down his life to take in his own body the punishment for our sins and for the sins of the entire world.

Key Scripture

John saw Jesus coming toward him and said, "Look, the Lamb of God, who takes away the sin of the world!" (John 1:29)

Christ Reveals His Name in Scripture

He was oppressed and afflicted,
   yet he did not open his mouth;
he was led like a lamb to the slaughter,
   and as a sheep before her shearers is silent,
   so he did not open his mouth. (Isaiah 53:7)

Now some Pharisees who had been sent questioned him, "Why then do you baptize if you are not the Christ, nor Elijah, nor the Prophet?"

"I baptize with water," John replied, "but among you stands one you do not know. He is the one who comes after me, the thongs of whose sandals I am not worthy to untie."

This all happened at Bethany on the other side of the Jordan, where John was baptizing.

The next day John saw Jesus coming toward him and said, "Look, the Lamb of God, who takes away the sin of the world! This is the one I meant when I said, 'A man who comes after me has surpassed me because he was before me.' I myself did not know him, but the reason I came baptizing with water was that he might be revealed to Israel."

Then John gave this testimony: "I saw the Spirit come down from heaven as a dove and remain on him. I would not have known him, except that the one who sent me to baptize with water told me, 'The man on whom you see the Spirit come down and remain is he who will baptize with the Holy Spirit.' I have seen and I testify that this is the Son of God."

The next day John was there again with two of his disciples. When he saw Jesus passing by, he said, "Look, the Lamb of God!" (John 1:24–35)

Understanding the Name

It is impossible to understand the title "Lamb of God" without understanding something about the practice of animal sacrifice in both Old and New Testaments. The sacrificial system provided a way for God's people to approach him even though they had violated the Mosaic law. When an animal was offered, its blood was shed and its flesh was then burned on the altar. When the animal was completely consumed by fire, the sacrifice was called a "holocaust." When only part of the animal was burned, it was considered a "peace offering," intended to restore communion with God. Those who offered sacrifices understood that the animal being sacrificed was a symbolic representation of themselves and their desire to offer their own lives to God. In fact, the sacrificial system of the Hebrew Scriptures represents God's way of instructing us about what it means to approach a holy God.

The lamb was the principal animal of sacrifice, and two were offered each day—one in the morning and one in the evening (Numbers 28:1–8). The offering was doubled on the Sabbath. Lambs (

blemishes.

The New Testament uses two Greek words for Christ as "Lamb" or "Lamb of God": *Arnion* (AR-nee-on) and *Amnos tou Theou* (am-NOS tou the-OU). The phrase "Lamb of God" is found only in John's gospel, though Jesus is often referred to as "the Lamb" in the book of Revelation, where he is portrayed as the Lamb who, though slain, yet lives and reigns victorious. In fact, twenty-nine of the thirty-four New Testament occurrences of "Lamb" are in Revelation, a book so named, at least in part, because of what it reveals about who God is. The New Testament also refers to Christ's followers as lambs.

When the temple was destroyed in AD 70, animal sacrifices could no longer be offered. Most Jews today no longer eat lamb during the Passover meal or Seder. Instead, they place a roasted lamb shank bone on a Seder plate as a reminder of the sacrifice.

Studying the Name

1. Jesus refused to defend himself when dragged before the Jewish leaders and before Pilate and Herod (Mark 14:53–65; 15:1–5). How does this relate to the passage from Isaiah? What does it say to you about Jesus?

2. Imagine that you are walking into the temple holding a young lamb in your arms. He is like a favorite pet, but now he is going to be sacrificed for your sins. How do you feel? Now imagine doing the same thing over and over because no one sacrifice can possibly take away your sins for all time. What thoughts go through your mind?

3. What comes to your mind when you think of Jesus as the Lamb of God? How does Jesus as the Lamb of God relate to your life?

4. Do you struggle to let go of guilt over your sins or failures? How might this make it difficult to accept God's forgiveness?

5. Why is belonging to Jesus, the Lamb of God, the only security capable of preserving us from death?

Passages for Continued Study

Genesis 22:6–13; Exodus 12:1–23, 46; John 19:31; Romans 8:31–36; 1 Corinthians 5:7b; 1 Peter 1:18–21; Revelation 5:6–10; 7:9–17; 12:10–11; 17:12–14; 19:6–9; 21:9–14

33

KING OF KINGS

βασιλεὺς βασιλέων

BASILEUS BASILEON

The world has never seen a king like Christ, a ruler mightier than any earthly sovereign and more powerful than the unseen powers of the universe. Though he entered the world humbly, as an infant born in Bethlehem, Magi from the east still recognized him as the newborn king. Though his reign unfolds in hidden ways, he has promised to come again, at which time he will reveal himself unambiguously as "King of kings and Lord of lords." When you pray to Jesus, the King of kings, call to mind his mastery not only over human beings but over nature, disease, and death itself.

Key Scripture

On his robe and on his thigh he has this name written:
KING OF KINGS AND LORD OF LORDS. (Revelation 19:16)

Christ Reveals His Name in Scripture

As they approached Jerusalem and came to Bethphage on the Mount of Olives, Jesus sent two disciples, saying to them, "Go to the village ahead of you, and at once you will find a donkey tied there, with her colt by her. Untie them and bring them to me. If anyone says anything to you, tell him that the Lord needs them, and he will send

brought the donkey and the colt, placed their cloaks on them, and Jesus sat on them. A very large crowd spread their cloaks on the road, while others cut branches from the trees and spread them on the road. The crowds that went ahead of him and those that followed shouted,

> "Hosanna to the Son of David!"
> "Blessed is he who comes in the name of the Lord!"
> "Hosanna in the highest!" (Matthew 21:1–9)

I saw heaven standing open and there before me was a white horse, whose rider is called Faithful and True. With justice he judges and makes war. His eyes are like blazing fire, and on his head are many crowns. He has a name written on him that no one knows but he himself. He is dressed in a robe dipped in blood, and his name is the Word of God. The armies of heaven were following him, riding on white horses and dressed in fine linen, white and clean. Out of his mouth comes a sharp sword with which to strike down the nations. "He will rule them with an iron scepter." He treads the winepress of the fury of the wrath of God Almighty. On his robe and on his thigh he has this name written:

KING OF KINGS AND LORD OF LORDS. (Revelation 19:11–16)

Understanding the Name

The Jewish people at the time of Christ longed for a coming king who would be descended from their great king, David. By hailing Jesus as the "Son of David," the large crowd who greeted him as he entered

Notes

Jerusalem was using a popular title for the Messiah. They expected their messianic king to restore Israel's freedom and former glory. In the passage from Matthew's gospel, Jesus fulfills the messianic prophecy of Zechariah 9:9 by riding into Jerusalem on a donkey, an animal that symbolized both peace and humility.

Today, Christ's kingdom unfolds in hidden ways as believers acknowledge him as King and Lord. But one day, when Christ comes again, his kingdom will be revealed as the greatest of all kingdoms. The passage from Revelation 19 presents Jesus riding not on a lowly donkey but on a magnificent white horse, as befits the greatest of all kings. Throughout the New Testament Jesus is variously referred to as "King," "King of the ages," "King of the Jews," "King of Israel," and "King of kings" — this last one translated from the Greek phrase *Basileus Basileon* (bas-si-LEUS ba-si-LE-own). Even today some Christian churches are called "basilicas," a phrase meaning "the hall of the king."

Studying the Name

1. Why do you think Scripture presents the reign of Jesus in two such different ways, as in the above passages?

3. What do you think it means to have Jesus as your king? How have you experienced his reign in your life thus far?

4. How can we "seek first the kingdom of God" in the midst of our lives today (see Matthew 6:33)?

5. What would life on earth look like today if Jesus' reign was perfectly established?

6. How would your own life look if Jesus' reign was perfectly established in you?

Passages for Continued Study

Matthew 6:9 – 10, 28 – 33; 24:9 – 14; 25:31 – 43; 27:27 – 37; Luke 17:22 – 25; 19:11 – 26; John 3:3 – 8; 1 Corinthians 6:9 – 11; 1 Timothy 6:11 – 16; 2 Peter 1:5 – 11; Revelation 11:15; 15:1 – 4; 17:12 – 14

34

PRINCE OF PEACE

Hebrew word for peace, however, means much more than the absence of conflict or the end of turmoil. *Shalom* conveys not only a sense of tranquility but also of wholeness and completion. To enjoy *shalom* is to enjoy health, satisfaction, success, safety, well-being, and prosperity. Though the New Testament does not directly call Jesus the Prince of Peace, this title from Isaiah has traditionally been associated with him as the one who brings peace to the world. Furthermore, Paul assured the Ephesian Christians saying of Jesus, "He himself is our peace" (Ephesians 2:14). When you pray to *Sar Shalom*, you are praying to Christ himself. To live in peace is to live in his presence.

Key Scripture

For to us a child is born,
*   to us a son is given,*
*   and the government will be on his shoulders.*
And he will be called
*   Wonderful Counselor, Mighty God,*
*   Everlasting Father, Prince of Peace. (Isaiah 9:6)*

Christ Reveals His Name in Scripture

The people walking in darkness
  have seen a great light;
on those living in the land of the shadow of death
  a light has dawned. . . .
For to us a child is born,
  to us a son is given,
  and the government will be on his shoulders.
And he will be called
  Wonderful Counselor, Mighty God,
  Everlasting Father, Prince of Peace.
Of the increase of his government and peace
  there will be no end.
He will reign on David's throne
  and over his kingdom,
establishing and upholding it
  with justice and righteousness
  from that time on and forever. (Isaiah 9:2, 6–7)

His [John's] father Zechariah was filled with the Holy Spirit and prophesied. . . .

"And you, my child, will be called a prophet of the Most High;
  for you will go on before the Lord to prepare the way for him,
to give his people the knowledge of salvation
  through the forgiveness of their sins,
because of the tender mercy of our God,
  by which the rising sun will come to us from heaven
to shine on those living in darkness
  and in the shadow of death,
to guide our feet into the path of peace." (Luke 1:67, 76–79)

Understanding the Name

Though the Hebrew title *Sar Shalom* (SAR sha-LOME) does not appear in the New Testament, the priest Zechariah calls it to mind with words that echo Isaiah 9. Both passages speak of a people living in darkness and in the shadow of death. And both speak of a child who will bring peace to God's people. Shortly after Christ was born, we hear angels proclaiming: "Glory to God in the highest heaven, and on earth peace to those on whom his favor rests" (Luke 2:14).

In Greek the word for peace is *eirene*. Like the Hebrew concept of *shalom*, the New Testament portrays peace as much more than the absence of conflict. Mark's gospel, for instance, links healing and peace by capturing Jesus' words to a woman he has just healed; he tells her to "go in peace" (Mark 5:34). The New Testament further develops our understanding of peace by revealing Jesus as the source of all peace. Though we were alienated from God because of our sins, Je...

Notes

Studying the Name

1. What does the word "peace" mean to you? How does this differ from the biblical idea of *shalom*?

2. Why is the "Prince of Peace" a fitting title for Jesus? Can you think of incidents in his life that display his peace?

3. What was the ultimate work of peace by Jesus? How has Jesus become our peace?

4. Ask yourself whether you are experiencing Christ's peace in your life. How can you participate more deeply in his peace?

5. Are there relationships in your life that cause conflict and strife? How might you bring the peace of God into these relationships?

6. What do you think it means to walk in "the path of peace"?

35

Christ, Messiah

Christos

Mashiach

Most of us are so familiar with the title "Christ" that we tend to consider it part of Jesus' personal name. But what exactly does it mean? Like "Messiah," "Christ" means the "anointed one." The phrase "anointed one" refers to someone who has been set apart for a special mission. That was how the first Christians thought about Jesus. As Israel's Messiah, he was the greatest of all kings, the one called and empowered to destroy God's enemies and extend his kingdom throughout the earth. His mission was to put an end to our deepest troubles—to rebellion, sin, and death. When we pray to Jesus Christ, we are praying to the Messiah, the Anointed One, whose mission involves calling the world back to God through the power of his love.

Key Scripture

Therefore let all Israel be assured of this: God has made this Jesus, whom you crucified, both Lord and Christ. (Acts 2:36)

Christ Reveals His Name in Scripture

"Listen to this: Jesus of Nazareth was a man accredited by God to you by miracles, wonders and signs, which God did among you through him, as you yourselves know. This man was handed over to you by God's set purpose and foreknowledge; and you, with the help of wicked men, put him to death by nailing him to the cross. But

When the people heard this, they were cut to the heart and said to Peter and the other apostles, "Brothers, what shall we do?"

Peter replied, "Repent and be baptized, every one of you, in the name of Jesus Christ for the forgiveness of your sins. And you will receive the gift of the Holy Spirit." (Acts 2:22–24, 32–33, 36–38)

Understanding the Name

Many ancient peoples believed that oil rubbed onto the body could impart strength, health, and beauty. Since oil was a staple of life in biblical times, used for lighting, cooking, medicine, cosmetic purposes, hygiene, and hospitality, it served as a symbol of both wealth and joy. An abundance of oil was evidence of God's pleasure; scarcity symbolized his displeasure.

Oil was also used for sacred purposes, such as consecrating altars and vessels for worship, indicating that they had been set apart for the Lord's purposes. People could also be anointed and set apart. Though some of Israel's high priests were anointed when they took office, Israel's kings, especially those descended from David, were anointed rather than crowned. According to rabbinic tradition, oil (olive oil mixed with spices like cinnamon, calamus, and myrrh) was poured on their heads in a circle to form a crown. This anointing signified the king's right to rule. It meant that God had blessed him with authority, strength, and honor.

When the prophet Samuel anointed David as king, David was also given the gift of the Spirit and accorded the Lord's special protection.

In time, oil became a symbol for the Holy Spirit, who imparts divine favor, power, and protection. The English word "christen" ("to anoint") comes from the Greek verb *chrio* ("to anoint").

The New Testament identifies Jesus as Christ, the "Anointed One," no less than 530 times. Jesus, however, was not anointed with oil but with the Holy Spirit at his baptism in the Jordan River. The early Christians understood that Jesus was the Christ—the Messiah, or *Mashiach* (ma-SHEE-ach)—in a unique sense. Like no king before him, he was called to heal the rift between God and his people.

Christ fulfilled his mission as the ideal king in a completely unexpected way, confounding his contemporaries, who expected the Messiah to be a powerful earthly king who would deliver Israel from its enemies. In order to avoid being forced into playing this political role, Jesus avoided the title of Christ or Messiah throughout most of his life. Finally, shortly before his death, he answered the high priest's question: "Are you the Christ, the Son of the Blessed One?" with the startling confession: "I am."

Studying the Name

1. Describe in your own words what it means to say that Jesus was anointed, or set apart for God's service.

3. What do you think it means to receive the gift of the Holy Spirit?

4. Why were the people who were listening to Jesus "cut to the heart"?

5. When have you experienced being cut to the heart by who Jesus is and what he has done for you?

6.   What do you think it means for believers to be anointed or set apart for Christ's service? How have you experienced this anointing in your own life?

Passages for Continued Study

Psalms 22; 69:20–21; Isaiah 11:1–9; 52; Zechariah 9:9; Matthew 16:13–23; Luke 24:45–48; John 12:1–7; Acts 2:22–38; Romans 8:32–37; 1 Corinthians 15:20–22; 2 Corinthians 1:18–22; 12:7–12; Galatians 3:26–28; Philippians 2:5–11; 3:7–14; 1 Peter 4:12–13

36

Rabbi, Rabbouni, Teacher

ῥαββί ῥαββουνί

DIDASKALOS

In Jesus' day, the name "rabbi" or "teacher" was normally reserved for someone who had studied under another rabbi for many years. Jesus offended the religious leaders of his day by ignoring this system. Instead of apprenticing himself to a rabbi, he simply laid down his carpenter tools and called twelve ordinary men to become his disciples. Unlike other rabbis, who merely passed on the teaching of the rabbi under whom they had studied, Jesus spoke with an authority that startled many of his listeners.

Two thousand years later, we are called to become his disciples, to stay as close to him as a disciple would to a rabbi, studying his life, examining his teaching, and allowing his Spirit to remake us in his image. When you pray to Rabbi Jesus, remember that you are praying to the only Teacher who is all-wise, all-good, and all-powerful, able to transform not only your mind but also your heart.

Key Scripture

[Jesus said to his disciples] "But you are not to be called 'Rabbi,'
for you have only one Master." (Matthew 23:8)

Christ Reveals His Name in Scripture

"But you are not to be called 'Rabbi,' for you have only one Master." (Matthew 23:8)

Jesus knew that the Father had put all things under his power, and that he had come from God and was returning to God; so he got up from the meal, took off his outer clothing, and wrapped a towel around his waist. After that, he poured water into a basin and began to wash his disciples' feet, drying them with the towel that was wrapped around him.

He came to Simon Peter, who said to him, "Lord, are you going to wash my feet?"

Jesus replied, "You do not realize now what I am doing, but later you will understand."

"No," said Peter, "you shall never wash my feet."

Jesus answered, "Unless I wash you, you have no part with me...."

When he had finished washing their feet, he put on his clothes and returned to his place. "Do you understand what I have done for you?" he asked them. "You call me 'Teacher' and 'Lord,' and rightly so, for that is what I am. Now that I, your Lord and Teacher, have washed your feet, you also should wash one another's feet. I have set you an example that you should do as I have done for you. I tell you the truth, no servant is greater than his master, nor is a messenger greater than the one who sent him. Now that you know these things, you will be blessed if you do them. (John 13:3–8, 12–17)

Understanding the Name

In ancient Israel all education was religious education, and Scripture was the sole textbook. Understanding it was vital, because long life, success, and happiness flowed from living in accordance with the laws of God. But the Jews did not believe that ordinary people were equipped to understand and apply Scripture without the guidance of a teacher. Gradually, scribes, who devoted their lives to copying and understanding the Mosaic law, became their primary instructors. Lacking access to the temple after the exile, the Jews began meeting together for prayer and instruction in places that became known as synagogues. Eventually, schools formed around these synagogues, where boys began to be educated between the ages of five and seven.

In the first century, "Rabbi" (ra-BEE, a Hebrew word) was used as a term of respect for teachers of the Scriptures. After AD 70 it became formalized as a title for scribes and theologians trained in the law. (*Rabbouni* [ra-BOU-nee] is an expanded Hebrew form that means "my rabbi.") Scribes were also known as "teachers of the law." The King James Version of the Bible calls them "lawyers."

members of the party of the Pharisees. Many of them, as Jesus pointed out, were consumed with the desire for public acclaim and positions of honor. Over time, the scribes added so many rules and regulations to the Law that Jesus faulted them for placing heavy burdens on the people without lifting a finger to help them.

Though Jesus' disciples called him "rabbi," which must have incensed the scribes because of his lack of formal training, there is no evidence he was ever ordained. Unlike most rabbis, who merely taught what they had learned from another rabbi, Jesus taught with his own authority, as though his wisdom came from above—a fact remarked upon by many who heard him. Jesus counseled his disciples never to seek the honorific title "rabbi." He alone was to be their Teacher and Master.

Another word for teacher in the New Testament is the Greek word *didaskalos* (di-DAS-ka-los). Jesus was an enormously popular teacher who drew crowds wherever he went, using questions, discussions, proverbs, symbolic actions, parables, and even miracles in order to teach people the way to live. The content of his teaching is most powerfully and eloquently evident in the story of his life.

Studying the Name

1. Why do you think Jesus cautioned his disciples in Matthew 23:8 against the title "rabbi"?

2. Why do you think Jesus washed his disciples' feet the night before his death, making this one of the last lessons he would leave them prior to his crucifixion?

3. Describe ways in which you have experienced people in leadership serving you.

4. How might God be calling you to serve in humble and hidden ways?

5. In Luke 6:40 Jesus said, "A student is not above his teacher, but everyone who is fully trained will be like his teacher." To whom do you look for counsel, guidance, and leadership? Whom do you work to emulate?

6. Do you avoid or resist certain difficult teachings of Christ? What are they?

Passages for Continued Study

Psalm 119:18; Matthew 7:21–29; 13:31–32; 19:16–21; 22:36–40; 23:8–12; Mark 8:22–25; John 9:1–3; 12:23–26; 14:15–18; 16:5–7, 12–15; 2 Timothy 3:16; James 1:5

37

WORD

λόγος

LOGOS

Though God has always revealed himself in some way, the incarnation is the clearest, most compelling revelation of who God is—of his holiness, love, and power. Because Jesus is one with the Father, he is uniquely able to communicate God's heart and mind. As *Logos*, or "the Word," everything about Jesus—his teaching, miracles, suffering, death, and resurrection—speaks to us of God. Our destiny depends on how well we listen. Will we believe, or will we turn a deaf ear to the message of God's love? When you pray to Jesus as the Word, you are praying to the one whose voice calls us from death to life and from darkness to light.

Key Scripture

The Word became flesh and made his dwelling among us.
We have seen his glory, the glory of the One and Only,
who came from the Father, full of grace and truth.
(John 1:14)

Christ Reveals His Name in Scripture

In the beginning was the Word, and the Word was with God, and the Word was God. He was with God in the beginning. Through him all things were made; without him nothing was made that has been made....

He was in the world, and though the world was made through him, the world did not recognize him. He came to that which was his

Understanding the Name

John's gospel begins by calling Jesus the *Logos* (LO-gos), the "Word." Though *Logos* was a term used in Greek philosophy, John echoes a Hebrew mindset by using it to refer not to a rational principle or an impersonal force but to the one who created the universe by speaking it into existence. Unlike the prophets, who merely *spoke* God's word, Jesus *is* God's dynamic, creative, life-giving Word.

Furthermore, John says, "The Word became flesh and made his dwelling among us" (John 1:14). The Greek for "made his dwelling" is linked to the word for "tent" or "tabernacle." Jewish readers would have immediately recognized this as a reference to the Tent of Meeting, in which God's glory dwelt prior to the building of the temple in Jerusalem. Jesus, the Word made flesh, became a man so that through his miracles, teachings, and way of life we could perceive God's glory. He is the Word calling out to us, healing our deafness and bringing us back to God.

No wonder Jesus responded to Philip by saying: "Don't you know me, Philip, even after I have been among you such a long time? Anyone who has seen me has seen the Father. How can you say, 'Show us the Father'? Don't you believe that I am in the Father, and that the Father is in me?" (John 14:9 – 10). We are to respond to Jesus, the Word, with both faith and faithfulness, reproducing Christ's life so that the Word may become flesh in us.

Studying the Name

1. Compare Genesis 1:1–5 with John 1:1–5. Why do you think John begins his gospel this way?

2. John says that though "the world was made through him, the world did not recognize him." Do you think this is still true today? Why or why not?

3. What does it mean to "believe in his name"?

4. John writes, "Yet to all who received him … he gave the right to become children of God." How does being a son or daughter of God shape the way you see yourself?

5. How hungry are you for the Word of God as spoken in the Bible? How do you express its value to you?

6.   What do you think it means to see God's glory?

38

CORNERSTONE, CAPSTONE

ἀκρογωνιαῖος λίθος

AKROGONIAIOS LITHOS

In the ancient world, stones were used for building altars, homes, palaces, and temples. When "capstone" or "cornerstone" is mentioned in the Bible, it refers to a particularly important stone that held two rows of stones together in a corner, one that stabilized the structure at the foundation, or a stone that formed the keystone over an arch or at the top of a roof parapet. In order to hold the structure together, the cornerstone had to be perfectly fitted for the task, both strong and well shaped. A flawed or poorly cut stone would compromise the building's integrity.

Jesus is the Cornerstone or Capstone to which we are joined as living stones. Together we form a spiritual house in which God can dwell. As the foundation stone on which God is building his kingdom, Jesus is strong enough to hold everything together. He is also the fitting conclusion to all God's work. When you pray to him as the Cornerstone, you are praying to the one on whom you can base your life.

Key Scripture

Jesus looked directly at them and asked, "Then what is the meaning
of that which is written: " 'The stone the builders rejected has become the capstone'?"
(Luke 20:17)

Christ Reveals His Name

He went on to tell the people this parable: "A man planted a vineyard, rented it to some farmers and went away for a long time. At harvest time he sent a servant to the tenants so they would give him some of the fruit of the vineyard. But the tenants beat him and sent him away empty-handed. He sent another servant, but that one also they beat and treated shamefully and sent away empty-handed. He sent still

come and kill those tenants and give the vineyard to others."

When the people heard this, they said, "May this never be!"

Jesus looked directly at them and asked, "Then what is the meaning of that which is written:

" 'The stone the builders rejected
      has become the capstone'?

"Everyone who falls on that stone will be broken to pieces, but he on whom it falls will be crushed."

The teachers of the law and the chief priests looked for a way to arrest him immediately, because they knew he had spoken this parable against them. But they were afraid of the people. (Luke 20:9 – 19)

Understanding the Name

When Jesus quoted the passage from Psalm 118:22, referring to the stone the builders rejected, he was pointing to his rejection by the Jewish nation and its leaders. But despite their rejection, God's purposes could not be thwarted. In fact, the Master Builder would make Jesus, through his death and resurrection, the *Akrogoniaios Lithos* (ah-kro-go-nee-EYE-os LI-thos), capstone or cornerstone, on which he would build his church. The New Testament portrays the whole community of believers as a holy temple in which God dwells. To those who reject Jesus and his saving message, he will be not a cornerstone but a stone of stumbling, because rejection of God's chosen one inevitably brings judgment.

As an interesting side note, a royal name was often inscribed on the cornerstone, and among the ancient Canaanites before the time of Joshua, the laying of the foundation stone was often accompanied by human sacrifice. Tragically, a number of skeletons, especially those of small babies in earthen jars, have been found at various sites.

Studying the Name

1. Why do you think Jesus' comments about "the stone the builders rejected" immediately follow the parable of the vineyard?

3. What do you think it means to build your life on Jesus as the Cornerstone?

4. How does basing your life on Jesus enable you to stand rather than collapse during times of unbearable pressure?

5. Which of your priorities need to shift in order for you to stand more squarely on Christ rather than trying to "stand" on insecure foundations like money, success, intelligence, relationships?

6. Picture yourself as a living stone being built into a spiritual house. How might this image affect your relationship with others in the church?

Passages for Continued Study

Psalms 18:2; 127:1; Isaiah 8:13–14; 28:16; Matthew 7:24–27; 24:1–2; Luke 19:41–44; John 2:13–20; Acts 3:1–4:12; Romans 9:30–32; 10:9, 13; 1 Corinthians 3:11; Ephesians 2:19–22; 1 Peter 2:4–9

39

BRIGHT MORNING STAR

ἀστὴρ λαμπρὸς

In the last chapter of Revelation, Jesus calls himself the "bright Morning Star." In ancient times, the morning star was thought of as a herald of the new day, signaling the dawn of hope and joy. The brightest object in the sky aside from the sun and moon, it is a fitting type for Christ, who ushers in a new day for the entire world. When you call on Jesus, the bright Morning Star, you are calling on the one from whom all darkness flees.

Key Scripture
"I am the Root and the Offspring of David, and the bright Morning Star."
(Revelation 22:16)

Christ Reveals His Name in Scripture

> I see him, but not now;
>   I behold him, but not near.
> A star will come out of Jacob;
>   a scepter will rise out of Israel. (Numbers 24:17)

"Behold, I am coming soon! My reward is with me, and I will give to everyone according to what they have done. I am the Alpha and the Omega, the First and the Last, the Beginning and the End.

"Blessed are those who wash their robes, that they may have the right to the tree of life and may go through the gates into the city. Outside are the dogs, those who practice magic arts, the sexually immoral, the murderers, the idolaters and everyone who loves and practices falsehood.

"I, Jesus, have sent my angel to give you this testimony for the churches. I am the Root and the Offspring of David, and the bright Morning Star." (Revelation 22:12–16)

Understanding the Name

What the Bible refers to as the morning star is actually the planet Venus, known since prehistoric times. As the second planet from the sun, it is also one of the hottest. A relatively young planet, it is Earth's closest neighbor and is often called our sister planet. Because of its appearance in the eastern sky before dawn, it was thought of as the harbinger of sunrise. The title *Aster Lampros Proinos* (as-TAIR lam-PROS pro-i-NOS) presents a powerful and beautiful image of the one who is also known as "the light of the world."

Studying the Name

1. Jesus says he is coming soon. In what ways do you think his second coming will differ from his first?

3. What kinds of people is Jesus describing in the passage from Revelation?

4. Throughout time, stars have been used by travelers as reference points. How does Jesus function as a reference point, our guiding star?

5. The writer to the Hebrews tells us to "fix our eyes on Jesus" (Hebrews 12:2). How will fixing your eyes on Jesus make a difference at times of adversity, confusion, fear, or temptation?

6. Stars shine in the darkness of night, but the morning star announces a new day. How does Jesus, the bright Morning Star, announce the dawn of a new day in your life and in the world?

Passages for Continued Study

Numbers 24:17; Psalm 139:11 – 12; Isaiah 29:18 – 19; Matthew 2:1 – 12; 16:2 – 3; Luke 1:67 – 79; Hebrews 1:3; 2 Peter 1:16 – 19; Revelation 2:26 – 28; 22:16

40

LION OF THE TRIBE OF JUDAH

אַרְיֵה לְמַטֵּה יְהוּדָה

Ἰούδα

LEON EK TES PHYLES IOUDA

Only once in the New Testament is Jesus described as a lion. The book of Revelation (named in part for what it reveals about Christ) portrays the risen Jesus as the only one worthy to open the scroll that contains the ultimate unfolding of God's purposes for the world. The apostle John perceived Jesus as both Lion and Lamb, who through his death and resurrection becomes the ultimate victor and conqueror. When you pray to Jesus as the Lion of the Tribe of Judah, you are praying to the one with the power to banish all fear, to the one who watches over you with his fierce protecting love. You are also praying to the one who is judge of the living and the dead.

Key Scripture

I wept and wept because no one was found who was worthy to open the scroll or look inside. Then one of the elders said to me, "Do not weep! See, the Lion of the tribe of Judah, the Root of David, has triumphed. He is able to open the scroll and its seven seals." (Revelation 5:4–5)

Christ Reveals His Name in Scripture

Judah, your brothers will praise you;
  your hand will be on the neck of your enemies;
  your father's sons will bow down to you.
You are a lion's cub, O Judah;
  you return from the prey, my son.
Like a lion he crouches and lies down,
  like a lioness — who dares to rouse him?
The scepter will not depart from Judah,
  nor the ruler's staff from between his feet,
until he comes to whom it belongs
  and the obedience of the nations is his. (Genesis 49:8 – 10)

Then I saw in the right hand of him who sat on the throne a scroll with writing on both sides and sealed with seven seals. And I saw a mighty angel proclaiming in a loud voice, "Who is worthy to break the seals and open the scroll?" But no one in heaven or on earth or under the earth could open the scroll or even look inside it. I wept and wept because no one was found who was worthy to open the scroll or look inside. Then one of the elders said to me, "Do not weep! See, the Lion of the tribe of Judah, the Root of David, has triumphed. He is able to open the scroll and its seven seals."

Then I saw a Lamb, looking as if it had been slain, standing in the center of the throne, encircled by the four living creatures and the elders. The Lamb had seven horns and seven eyes, which are the seven spirits of God sent out into all the earth. He went and took the scroll from the right hand of him who sat on the throne. And when he had taken it, the four living creatures and the twenty-four elders fell down before the Lamb. Each one had a harp and they were holding golden bowls full of incense, which are the prayers of God's people. And they sang a new song, saying:

"You are worthy to take the scroll
  and to open its seals,
because you were slain,
  and with your blood you purchased for God
  members of every tribe and language and people and nation.
You have made them to be a kingdom and priests to serve our God,
  and they will reign on the earth." (Revelation 5:1 – 10)

Understanding the Name

Today, lions can be found in sub-Saharan Africa and in northwest India. But in biblical times lions also roamed the region of the world now comprised of Israel, Syria, Iran, Iraq, Greece, and Turkey. From ancient times their images have graced thrones, palaces, gates, and temples, including the temple in Jerusalem. First Kings 10 indicates that King Solomon's throne was adorned with twelve lions, one on each end of the six steps leading up to it.

Though lions are sometimes a symbol of evil, they are also used as symbols of God's people. Near the end of his life, the patriarch Jacob prayed a blessing over his twelve sons. When it came time to bless Judah, he compared him to a lion—hence the phrase "the Lion of the Tribe of Judah" (*Aryeh Lammatteh Yehudah* in Hebrew, pronounced ar-YEH la-mat-TEH ye-hou-DAH, or *Leon ek tes Phyles Iouda*, in Greek, pronounced LE-own ek teys fu-LAIS YOU-dah). Jacob's prediction that the scepter would not depart from Judah has been traditionally applied to the Messiah.

In the Hebrew Scriptures, *Yahweh* is sometimes depicted as a lion who roars in judgment against the nations and against his own faithless people. But he is also depicted as a mighty lion who fights fiercely on behalf of his people. Revelation depicts the risen Christ as the mightiest of all victors. He is the Lion of the Tribe of Judah, the one found worthy to open the scrolls of history; this means that he is in charge of history and of how the world's destiny unfolds.

Studying the Name

1. Why do you think the book of Revelation portrays Jesus as both Lion and Lamb?

2. In the Bible "seven" is considered a sacred number, symbolizing perfection or completeness, while a "horn" symbolizes power. What does this say to you about how the Lamb is portrayed in Revelation 5?

3. How have you experienced and understood both the "lamblike" and "lionlike" nature of Jesus in your own life?

4. What does it mean for us "to be a kingdom and priests to serve our God"?

5. The Lion of the Tribe of Judah, the ultimate victor and conqueror, has the power to banish all fear and to watch over you with fierce, protective love. Picture this literally, then describe how this promise of safety might affect the way you face your fears.

6. What specific victories has Christ already won in your life?

Passages for Continued Study

Psalm 106:8; Proverbs 19:12; 28:1; Isaiah 11:6–9; 31:4–5; Hosea 11:9–11; Joel 3:16; Amos 3:6–8; Matthew 27:50–54; John 3:36; Revelations 5:5–6

41

LORD

κύριος

KYRIOS

Christianity's earliest confession of faith consisted of three short but incredibly powerful words: *Jesus is Lord!* The early Christians believed that the Father had placed Jesus, by virtue of his death and resurrection, at the apex of time and eternity—higher than any power or person in the universe. It is no wonder that Paul was "convinced that neither death nor life, neither angels nor demons, neither the present nor the future, nor any powers, neither height nor depth, nor anything else in all creation, will be able to separate us from the love of God that is in Christ Jesus our Lord" (Romans 8:38–39). Both those who love him and those who oppose him will one day call Jesus "Lord." In the end, even the devil will be forced to acknowledge him.

As you bow your head in prayer before the sovereign Lord, remember that you are placing your life—the worst of your disappointments, the most protracted of your struggles, the wildest of your dreams—squarely in his hands. Knowing Jesus as Lord will lead you to a deeper experience of his presence and his power.

Key Scripture

Therefore God exalted him to the highest place
and gave him the name that is above every name,
that at the name of Jesus every knee should bow,
in heaven and on earth and under the earth,
and every tongue confess that Jesus Christ is Lord,
to the glory of God the Father. (Philippians 2:9–11)

Christ Reveals His Name

Your attitude should be the same as that of Christ Jesus:

Who, being in very nature God,
    did not consider equality with God something to be grasped,
but made himself nothing,
    taking the very nature of a servant,

and every tongue confess that Jesus Christ is Lord,
    to the glory of God the Father. (Philippians 2:5–11)

Understanding the Name

The Greek word *Kyrios* (KU-ree-os) is used in the New Testament to refer to an owner, emperor, king, father, husband, or master. It can also translate three Hebrew names and titles of God: *Yahweh, Adonai,* and *Elohim.* When people addressed Jesus as *Kyrios* or "Lord" in the Gospels, they were often simply showing respect to him as a rabbi or teacher, addressing him as "sir" rather than acknowledging him as the Lord God. But after his death and resurrection, the title "Lord" began to be widely used by believers in a more specialized sense.

Remember the apostle Thomas, who at first doubted accounts of Christ's resurrection? When Jesus appeared to him after his death, Thomas instinctively responded with a confession of faith, saying: "My Lord and my God!" (John 20:28). Over time, the title "Lord" began to take on the characteristics of a name. As such, it clearly identifies Jesus with *Yahweh,* the covenant name of God in the Hebrew Scriptures. Of the 717 passages in which *Kyrios* occurs in the New Testament, the majority are found in Luke's gospel, the book of Acts, and Paul's writings.

Studying the Name

1. How did God the Father respond to Jesus' willing obedience, even to death on a cross?

2. What do you think it means that every tongue will confess that Jesus Christ is Lord?

3. How does God's idea of greatness differ from the usual definition?

4. Have you been reserving any part of your life — a relationship, habit, dream, or concern — because you fear what the Lord may ask of you?

5. How have you experienced Jesus being Lord in your life?

Passages for Continued Study

Deuteronomy 10:14 – 17; Matthew 7:21; Mark 10:42 – 45; Luke 2:8 – 14; 5:4 – 8; John 20:24 – 29; Ephesians 5:8 – 10; Philippians 2:5 – 11; 4:4; 2 Peter 3:8 – 10; Romans 14:10 – 12; 16:12

42

FRIEND

φίλος

PHILOS

Jesus is not only Lord and Master but the greatest of all friends, who willingly proved his friendship by his death on the cross. By this costly gesture he has won the friendship of millions of men and women from every tongue and tribe and nation. When you pray to Jesus your Friend, you are praying to the one who loved you before you were loveable and the one who links you together with his many friends throughout the world.

Key Scripture

Greater love has no one than this: to lay down one's life for one's friends.
(John 15:13)

Christ Reveals His Name in Scripture

As the Father has loved me, so have I loved you. Now remain in my love. If you keep my commands, you will remain in my love, just as I have kept my Father's commands and remain in his love. I have told you this so that my joy may be in you and that your joy may be complete. My command is this: Love each other as I have loved you. Greater love has no one than this: to lay down one's life for one's

died for the ungodly. Very rarely will anyone die for a righteous person, though for a good person someone might possibly dare to die. But God demonstrates his own love for us in this: While we were still sinners, Christ died for us.

Since we have now been justified by his blood, how much more shall we be saved from God's wrath through him! For if, when we were God's enemies, we were reconciled to him through the death of his Son, how much more, having been reconciled, shall we be saved through his life! Not only is this so, but we also boast in God through our Lord Jesus Christ, through whom we have now received reconciliation. (Romans 5:6–11)

Understanding the Name

The Greek word *philos* (FEE-los) means "friend" or "relative." Occurring twenty-eight times in the New Testament, it is also used to describe the close relationship that exists among believers, related to each other by virtue of their faith in Jesus. This word is related to *phileo*, the most general term for "to love" in the New Testament, and to the word *philema*, which means "a kiss." In fact, the early Christians used to greet each other with a holy kiss, signifying their close relationship.

John's gospel indicates that Jesus not only called his disciples his friends but defined his own relationship with them by what was to be the greatest of all acts of friendship, in which he would lay down his

Notes

life for them. Furthermore, unlike most men of his day, Jesus had both male and female friends. Luke addressed his gospel to someone named *Theophilus*, a proper name meaning "friend of God." The designation "friends" has survived as another name for those who belong to the religious group known as Quakers.

Studying the Name

1. What is the command that allows us to remain in Jesus' love? Why do you think that Jesus made this the key?

3. Describe the difference between being a servant of God and becoming a true friend of Jesus.

4. Describe the best friendship you have ever had. How does it compare with the way you have experienced Jesus' friendship?

5. How can you deepen your friendship with Christ?

6. If Jesus died for us while we were still his enemies, as Romans 5:6–11 tells us, how should we regard our own enemies?

Passages for Continued Study

Exodus 33:7–11; Job 29:2–6; Proverbs 17:17; 18:24; 27:6, 9; Ecclesiastes 4:9–12; Matthew 11:19; 26:47–51; Luke 5:17–20; John 11:1–44; 21:4–7; James 2:20–24; 4:4–10

43

ALPHA AND OMEGA

ἄλφα καὶ Ὦ

the First and the Last, the Beginning and the End." Present at the world's beginning, Jesus will also be present at its end, when he and his work are finally and fully revealed. When you pray to Christ as the Alpha and the Omega, you are praying to the one who is, who was, and who is to come. He is our all-sufficient Lord, who will not fail to complete the good work he has begun in us.

Key Scripture
"I am the Alpha and the Omega, the First and the Last,
the Beginning and the End."
(Revelation 22:13)

Christ Reveals His Name in Scripture

> Listen to me, O Jacob,
>   Israel, whom I have called:
> I am he;
>   I am the first and I am the last. (Isaiah 48:12)

> He who was seated on the throne said, "I am making everything new!" Then he said, "Write this down, for these words are trustworthy and true."
> He said to me: "It is done. I am the Alpha and the Omega, the Beginning and the End." (Revelation 21:5 – 6)
> "Behold, I am coming soon! My reward is with me, and I will give to everyone according to what they have done. I am the Alpha and the Omega, the First and the Last, the Beginning and the End." (Revelation 22:12 – 13)

Understanding the Name

The title "Alpha and Omega" occurs only three times in the Bible, and all three are in the book of Revelation. Because *Alpha* and *Omega* are the first and last letters in the Greek alphabet, Revelation 22:13 could be paraphrased: "I am the A and the Z, the First and the Last, the Beginning and the End." These verses in Revelation probably allude to passages in Isaiah in which God identifies himself as being both the first and the last (Isaiah 44:6; 48:12).

Studying the Name

1. Can you imagine a human being claiming to be the A to Z? Why or why not?

3. How do you think this title relates to Christ's divinity?

4. What would it mean to say that Jesus is first and last in your own life?

5. Instead of looking at your life as *your story*, what if you viewed your life as part of *God's story*? What implications does this have for the way you live and the goals you have?

6. "In him we live and move and have our being" (Acts 17:28). What does this mean to you?

Passages for Continued Study

Psalm 113:1–3; Isaiah 44:6; Daniel 7:9–13; John 1:1–3; 8:54–58; Philippians 1:3–6; Colossians 1:15–20; Hebrews 12:2; 13:8; Revelation 1:7–8, 12–13, 17–18; 21:1–7

44

JESUS THE SAVIOR

Ἰησοῦς σωτήρ

the personal name of the one we call Redeemer, Lord, and Savior. Her name is
intimately linked to the God of the Hebrew Scriptures because it means "*Yahweh
Is Salvation.*" Indeed, Jesus is *Yahweh* come to earth. If you have ever pictured
God as a distant, wrathful Being, you will have to reconsider that portrait in light
of Jesus Christ, who is God bending toward us, God becoming one of us, God
reaching out in mercy, God humbling himself, God nailed to a cross, God rising
up from the grave to show us the way home. Jesus, name above all names, beautiful Savior, glorious Lord!

Key Scripture

Joseph son of David, do not be afraid to take Mary home as your wife,
because what is conceived in her is from the Holy Spirit.
She will give birth to a son, and you are to give him the name Jesus,
because he will save his people from their sins.
(Matthew 1:20–21)

Christ Reveals His Name in Scripture

This is how the birth of Jesus Christ came about: His mother Mary was pledged to be married to Joseph, but before they came together, she was found to be with child through the Holy Spirit. Because Joseph her husband was a righteous man and did not want to expose her to public disgrace, he had in mind to divorce her quietly.

But after he had considered this, an angel of the Lord appeared to him in a dream and said, "Joseph son of David, do not be afraid to take Mary home as your wife, because what is conceived in her is from the Holy Spirit. She will give birth to a son, and you are to give him the name Jesus, because he will save his people from their sins."

All this took place to fulfill what the Lord had said through the prophet: "The virgin will be with child and will give birth to a son, and they will call him Immanuel"—which means, "God with us."

When Joseph woke up, he did what the angel of the Lord had commanded him and took Mary home as his wife. But he had no union with her until she gave birth to a son. And he gave him the name Jesus. (Matthew 1:18–25)

Understanding the Name

Luke's gospel tells us that Mary's infant was given the name "Jesus" at the time of his circumcision, a name given him by the angel Gabriel when he appeared to Mary (Luke 1:31; 2:21).

"Jesus" was a common name in first-century Palestine, and it has been found on various grave markers and tombs in and around Jerusalem. The full name of Barabbas, the insurrectionist Pilate released instead of Jesus, was probably Jesus Barabbas. To distinguish him from others of the same name, Jesus is sometimes referred to in the Gospels as Jesus of Nazareth, Jesus the son of Joseph, or Jesus the Nazarene. Later on, particularly in Acts and the New Testament letters, he is referred to as "Jesus Christ," as though Christ is his surname. By the second century the name "Jesus" had become so closely associated with Jesus of Nazareth that it nearly disappeared as a name given to either Christians or Jews.

The name "Jesus" (in English) or *Iesous* (in Greek) is the equivalent of the Hebrew "*Yeshua*," itself a contraction of the Hebrew name "*Yehoshua*," translated "Joshua" in English Bibles. The name Joshua is the oldest name containing *Yahweh*, the covenant name of God, a name so sacred it was considered too holy to pronounce. Both "Jesus" and "Joshua" mean "*Yahweh* Is Help" or "*Yahweh* Is Salvation." *Yeshua* is also related to the word *yeshu'ah*, which means "salvation."

"*Soter*" is the Greek word translated "Savior." Its Hebrew equivalent is *Moshia*. In Greek, "Jesus the Savior" is rendered *Iesous Soter* (yay-SOUS so-TAIR). Through the centuries, the church has affirmed the belief of the earliest followers of Jesus that "salvation is found in no one else, for there is no other name given under heaven by which we

Studying the Name

1. What comes to mind when you hear the name "Jesus"?

2. Though "Jesus" was a common name in first-century Palestine, God sent an angel to announce the name to Joseph. Comment on the significance of this.

3. Describe what Joseph might have thought and felt when the angel said that this baby would save God's people from their sin.

4. In what circumstances in your life do you need to proclaim the powerful, saving name of Jesus?

5. Why do you think Jesus' name is linked to the name of *Yahweh*, the covenant name of God in the Hebrew Scriptures?

6.   Describe what salvation means to you.

45

BRIDEGROOM, HUSBAND

NYMPHIOS

ANER

God is not content to be known merely as Creator, Lord, or even Father. Incredibly he reveals himself also as Bridegroom or Husband. The Hebrew Scriptures contain numerous allusions to *Yahweh* as Israel's divine Husband, and the New Testament presents Christ as the church's Bridegroom. He is the Holy One who did not cling to his divinity but left his Father's house to dwell among us, calling us to become one with him in the most intimate way possible. To all of us, male and female, Christ offers himself as our Provider and Protector, the one who has forever pledged himself in faithfulness and love.

Key Scripture

Blessed are those who are invited to the wedding supper of the Lamb!
(Revelation 19:9)

Christ Reveals His Name in Scripture

"For your Maker is your husband—
  the LORD Almighty is his name—
the Holy One of Israel is your Redeemer;
  he is called the God of all the earth.
The LORD will call you back

rushing waters and like loud peals of thunder, shouting:

"Hallelujah!
  For our Lord God Almighty reigns.
Let us rejoice and be glad
  and give him glory!
For the wedding of the Lamb has come,
  and his bride has made herself ready.
Fine linen, bright and clean,
  was given her to wear."

(Fine linen stands for the righteous acts of the saints.)

Then the angel said to me, "Write: 'Blessed are those who are invited to the wedding supper of the Lamb!'" And he added, "These are the true words of God." (Revelation 19:6–9)

Understanding the Name

Marriage in Israel was generally considered sacred, the only acceptable state of life for men and women. Despite polygamous practices, whereby a man could marry more than one wife, monogamy was the accepted pattern throughout most of biblical history, especially after the patriarchal period.

Most marriages were arranged by parents. The minimum age for girls was twelve and for boys was thirteen. The period of engagement or betrothal usually lasted a year and was considered so binding that a man who had intimate relations with a virgin betrothed to another man would be stoned. For the year following the marriage, the husband was exempt from military service. This practice prevented the bride from becoming a widow in her first year of marriage and it also allowed the man to devote himself more fully to his wife at the start of their marriage.

Though the marriage ceremony itself was brief, the celebration surrounding it could be elaborate, consisting of seven and sometimes fourteen days of feasting and celebrating. During the festivities, dating from the time of Solomon, both bride and groom were crowned as king and queen and their virtues were extolled in song and poetry.

The Hebrew Scriptures did not hesitate to describe the relationship between God and his people in the most intimate of terms: *Yahweh* was the husband of Israel, his not-so-faithful wife. By referring to himself as the bridegroom, Jesus was clearly linking himself with *Yahweh.* New Testament writers presented the church as the bride of Christ. *Nymphios* (num-FEE-os) is the Greek word for "bridegroom" or "young husband" while *aner (*an-AIR*)* can be translated "man" or "husband."

When the disciples of John the Baptist asked Jesus why his disciples did not fast, Jesus replied that it was not possible for the guests of the bridegroom to mourn as long as he was with them (Matthew 9:14 – 15). John the Baptist used similar imagery when he referred to himself as the "friend who attends the bridegroom" — that is, the best man (John 3:29).

Studying the Name

1. What does the passage from Isaiah reveal about God's character?

3. How does the passage from Revelation compare and contrast with the passage from Isaiah?

4. Describe why the Bible is best understood not as a rule book or a compendium of wisdom but as a love story.

5. How have you experienced God protecting and providing for you as a loving husband?

6. In what ways might you spurn the love of Jesus? What pulls you away from him? What tempts you to look elsewhere for help, hope, and fulfillment?

Passages for Continued Study

Song of Songs; Isaiah 61:10 – 62:5; Jeremiah 3:14 – 17, 20; Hosea 2:13 – 3:1; Matthew 22:1 – 14; 25:1 – 13; John 14:1 – 3; Romans 7:1 – 6; 1 Corinthians 13:12; Ephesians 5:15 – 32; Revelation 21:1 – 3, 9 – 27; 22:1 – 17

46

SON OF DAVID

υἱὸς Δαυίδ

very heart of God. So it may not be surprising that the ...

begins and ends with references to Jesus as the Son or Offspring of David. He is the one who fulfilled the promise of a coming King so beloved by God that his throne will endure forever. Like David, Jesus was born in Bethlehem (the city of David). And like David, who established his kingdom by overcoming Israel's enemies and uniting God's people, Jesus established his kingdom by defeating the principalities and powers, making a way for us to become part of it as we confess our faith in him. When you pray to Jesus as the Son of David, you are praying to the long-awaited King, human by virtue of his descent from David and divine by virtue of being God's only Son.

Key Scripture

The Lord God will give him the throne of his father David, and he will reign over the house of Jacob forever; his kingdom will never end. (Luke 1:32–33)

Christ Reveals His Name in Scripture

"Now then, tell my servant David, 'This is what the LORD Almighty says: I took you from the pasture and from following the flock, to be ruler over my people Israel. I have been with you wherever you have gone, and I have cut off all your enemies from before you. Now I will make your name like the names of the greatest men of the earth. And I will provide a place for my people Israel and will plant them so that they can have a home of their own and no longer be disturbed. Wicked people will not oppress them anymore, as they did at the beginning and have done ever since the time I appointed leaders over my people Israel. I will also subdue all your enemies.

"'I declare to you that the LORD will build a house for you: When your days are over and you go to be with your fathers, I will raise up your offspring to succeed you, one of your own sons, and I will establish his kingdom. He is the one who will build a house for me, and I will establish his throne forever. I will be his father, and he will be my son. I will never take my love away from him, as I took it away from your predecessor. I will set him over my house and my kingdom forever; his throne will be established forever.'" (1 Chronicles 17:7–14)

In the sixth month, God sent the angel Gabriel to Nazareth, a town in Galilee, to a virgin pledged to be married to a man named Joseph, a descendant of David. The virgin's name was Mary. The angel went to her and said, "Greetings, you who are highly favored! The Lord is with you."

Mary was greatly troubled at his words and wondered what kind of greeting this might be. But the angel said to her, "Do not be afraid, Mary, you have found favor with God. You will be with child and give birth to a son, and you are to give him the name Jesus. He will be great and will be called the Son of the Most High. The Lord God will give him the throne of his father David, and he will reign over the house of Jacob forever; his kingdom will never end." (Luke 1:26–33)

Understanding the Name

The New Testament tells a story that cannot be adequately understood without reference to the Old Testament. Though composed of many books written at different times by different authors, much of the Bible is a continuing narrative that tells the story of salvation in ever-deepening detail. One of the ways it does this is by encapsulating the story or part of the story in the life of a particular person in the

Bible whose shadow is then cast forward across the remaining pages of the Bible.

David is certainly one of these characters, for in many ways his life prefigures the life of Christ. Like Christ, David conquered against incredible odds. Like Christ, he was beloved of God. And like Christ, he was a warrior king who defeated God's enemies. David began as a shepherd boy signifying Jesus' coming role as the good Shepherd who

refers to Jesus as the "Root and Offspring of David," the "descendant" or "seed" of David, and the one who holds the "key of David." Along with acknowledging Jesus as the rightful heir to David's throne, the title "Son of David" also locates Jesus within a human genealogy, that of Abraham and David.

Studying the Name

1. Do you think the prophecy recounted in 1 Chronicles was fulfilled in the life of David's son Solomon? Why or why not? (See 1 Kings 10:26–11:13.)

2. Compare the lives of Jesus and David. What similarities do you see? What differences?

3. Consider how different life might be if you lived under a corrupt or incompetent government. Now think of how different life might be if you lived in a country that was perfectly governed, ruled by a leader who was all-powerful, all-wise, and all-loving. Describe the differences.

4. What difficulties do you face? What would happen if you saw every difficulty as an opportunity for Jesus, as the Son of David, to extend his rule over you?

5. What areas of your life are not yet fully under Christ's rule? What specific things could you do right now to change that?

6. What do you think it means to be a man or woman "after God's own heart"? How is God's heart already manifested in you?

47

PRIEST, PROPHET

ἱερεύς

HIEREUS

προφήτης

PROPHETES

Jesus is both Priest—the one who faithfully bears us into God's presence by virtue of his self-sacrifice—and Prophet—the one who perfectly communicates God's Word to us. We are called to listen to him, to trust in his work, and to take our places as part of a kingdom of priests, who in Christ Jesus offer ourselves on behalf of others. As you pray to Jesus as both Priest and Prophet, ask him to help you understand the deep meaning of these titles so that you can live out their truths in your life.

Key Scriptures

Therefore, since we have a great high priest who has gone through the heavens, Jesus the Son of God, let us hold firmly to the faith we profess.
(Hebrews 4:14)

In the past God spoke to our ancestors through the prophets at many times and in various ways, but in these last days he has spoken to us by his Son.
(Hebrews 1:1–2a)

Christ Reveals His Name in Scripture

Therefore, since we have a great high priest who has gone through the heavens, Jesus the Son of God, let us hold firmly to the faith we profess. For we do not have a high priest who is unable to sympathize with our weaknesses, but we have one who has been tempted in every way, just as we are — yet was without sin. Let us then approach the throne of grace with confidence, so that we may receive mercy and find

them a prophet like you from among their brothers; I will put my words in his mouth, and he will tell them everything I command him." (Deuteronomy 18:15 – 18)

In the past God spoke to our ancestors through the prophets at many times and in various ways, but in these last days he has spoken to us by his Son, whom he appointed heir of all things, and through whom also he made the universe. The Son is the radiance of God's glory and the exact representation of his being, sustaining all things by his powerful word. (Hebrews 1:1 – 3)

Understanding the Name

Prophet, priest, and king — these were the three major offices in Israel, titles also ascribed to Jesus. While the king governed as God's representative on earth, the priest's role was to represent the people to God by offering sacrifices, prayers, and praise on their behalf. Unlike kings and priests, which were normally hereditary offices held only by males, prophets had to be commissioned by God, and they could be either male or female.

The role of the priest was to bring the people before God. Moses' brother, Aaron, was the first Israelite priest. Thereafter priests were drawn from among his descendants, and they were given charge of worship, which eventually became centralized in the Jerusalem temple. Unlike worship in many churches today, Jewish worship primarily consisted not in singing songs and listening to sermons but in offering sacrifices as prescribed by the Mosaic law. The priest's role was to offer sacrifices for his own sins and for the sins of the people. The animals killed for this purpose served as a continual reminder to both priests and people that the penalty for sin is death.

The priesthood consisted of three groups: the high priest, ordinary priests, and Levites. The Levites occupied the lowest rung of the ladder, taking care of the temple service. The priests, who alone could offer sacrifices, were next. At the pinnacle stood the high priest, the only one authorized to enter the Most Holy Place on the Day of Atonement. On his ephod (a garment attached to the breast piece) were stones that bore the names of the twelve tribes of Israel, a physical reminder that the high priest was bearing the people into God's presence.

The New Testament identifies Jesus as a priest according to the order of Melchizedek (Melchizedek, a priest who was a contemporary of Abraham, predated the Levites). This was a way of indicating that his priesthood was both different from and superior to that of the Levitical priesthood. Though most priests in Jerusalem at the time of Jesus rejected him, the book of Hebrews, emphasizing Jesus' role as High Priest, may have been aimed primarily at priests who became believers after the resurrection. The Greek word for "priest" is *hierus* (hee-eh-REUS).

While the primary role of the priest was to speak to God on behalf of the people, the prophet's primary responsibility was to speak to the people on behalf of God. The great prophets of the Hebrew Scriptures included Moses, Isaiah, Jeremiah, Elijah, and Elisha. While prophets sometimes predicted future events, more often they called people to faithfulness.

Jesus acknowledged that his cousin, John, was a prophet—and more than a prophet because he prophesied most clearly about the Messiah. Though the common people acclaimed Jesus as a prophet and though he seemed comfortable with this title, most of the priests rejected this title for Jesus. In a Jewish context, Jesus' baptism in the Jordan, when the Spirit descended on him, would have been understood as a time in which he was commissioned by God as a prophet. But unlike the prophets who preceded him, Jesus would be the one Prophet who not only perfectly revealed God's Word but who perfectly revealed God himself.

The New Testament identifies several people besides John the Baptist as prophets or as people who prophesied at one time or another. These included John's father, Zechariah; Elizabeth; Simeon; Anna; the high priest Caiphas; Agabus; and Barnabas. The New Testament also indicates that there were prophets in the early church and that prophecy was considered one of the spiritual gifts. The Greek word *prophetes* (pro-PHAY-tays) is found 144 times in the New Testament, which, in proportion to its length, contains as many references to prophets and prophecies as do the Hebrew Scriptures.

Studying the Name

1. Why do you think it is important that Jesus, as High Priest, is able to sympathize with our weakness?

2. What about Jesus made him capable of sympathizing with us?

3. The role of a priest is to bring people before God and to speak to God on their behalf. How has Jesus performed this role in your life?

4. Why do you think Jesus was more effective than the priests of the Old Testament?

5. A prophet's job is to speak to the people on behalf of God. How has Jesus fulfilled this role in your life?

6.   What do you think it means that "the Son is the radiance of God's glory" (Hebrews 1:3)?

48

SON OF GOD, SON OF MAN

υἱὸς τοῦ θεοῦ

HUIOS TOU THEOU

υἱὸς τοῦ ἀνθρώπου

HUIOS TOU ANTHROPOU

Like the Father, Jesus is God. He always was, always is, and always will be. But unlike the Father, Jesus is also a human being. Though charged with blasphemy and crucified for claiming to be one with the Father, Jesus' resurrection validates his claim to be God's Son in a unique way. When we confess our belief that Jesus is the Son of God, we share in the love the Father has for the Son, becoming adopted children of God.

Though Jesus was the Son of God, he was also the Son of Man, a title that emphasizes both his lowliness and his eventual dominion. Near the end of his life, when the high priest asked him whether he was the Son of God, Jesus no longer avoided the title but said that he would one day "see the Son of Man sitting at the right hand of the Mighty One and coming on the clouds of heaven" (Matthew 26:64). When you pray to Jesus as Son of God and Son of Man, you are praying to the One who is your Brother and your Lord.

Key Scripture

"But what about you?" he asked. "Who do you say I am?"
Simon Peter answered, "You are the Messiah, the Son of the living God."
Jesus replied, "Blessed are you, Simon son of Jonah, for this was not revealed to you
by flesh and blood, but by my Father in heaven." (Matthew 16:15–17)

Christ Reveals His Name in Scripture

In my vision at night I looked, and there before me was one like a son of man, coming with the clouds of heaven. He approached the Ancient of Days and was led into his presence. He was given authority, glory and sovereign power; all nations and peoples of every language worshiped him. His dominion is an everlasting dominion that will not pass away, and his kingdom is one that will never be destroyed. (Daniel

Jesus replied, "Blessed are you, Simon son of Jonah, for this was not revealed to you by flesh and blood, but by my Father in heaven. And I tell you that you are Peter, and on this rock I will build my church, and the gates of death will not overcome it. I will give you the keys of the kingdom of heaven; whatever you bind on earth will be bound in heaven, and whatever you loose on earth will be loosed in heaven." Then he ordered his disciples not to tell anyone that he was the Messiah.

From that time on Jesus began to explain to his disciples that he must go to Jerusalem and suffer many things at the hands of the elders, the chief priests and the teachers of the law, and that he must be killed and on the third day be raised to life. (Matthew 16:13–21)

Understanding the Name

Though the phrase "sons of God" was occasionally used in the Hebrew Scriptures, the Greek phrase "Son of God," *Huios tou Theou* (hui-OS tou the-OU) belongs to Jesus in a unique way. Jesus himself indicates that he and the Father are one. He is the only man who could bear the title without dishonoring the Father.

But Jesus is God's Son not in the sense that most Westerners think of sonship, as though the Father preexisted him. Instead, Jesus is God's Son in the sense that he shares his nature and represents his intentions. He is fully divine and therefore perfectly capable of representing the Father on earth. Twice in the Gospels—at Jesus' baptism and at the transfiguration—a voice from heaven announced: "This is my Son, whom I love."

During Jesus' earthly ministry, even the demons recognized Christ as the "Son of God." However, it was this politically charged title that led to Jesus' death, which may be why he avoided it until the end of his life. Recognizing this as a primary title of Christ, the early church baptized those who confessed Jesus Christ as the Son of God. These early believers understood, as we do, that our relationship with Christ enables us to become adopted children of the Father.

Though Jesus was the Son of God, his favorite title for himself was the "Son of Man," *Huios tou Anthropou* (hui-OS tou an-THROW-pou). It's a somewhat enigmatic title. But certainly a primary meaning of it is that Jesus is the perfect Human Being. He shows us through his life on earth what men and women were intended by God to be before we fell prey to sin. But the title also has messianic connotations and is closely connected with Jesus' second coming.

Together the titles Son of Man and Son of God express the incredible mystery of the incarnation—that the second person of the Trinity came down from heaven to become one of us so that we could be one with him. When Jesus rose from the dead, he ascended into heaven, not just as God but also as a man. C. S. Lewis remarked on this truth: "I seldom meet any strong or exultant sense of the continued, never-to-be-abandoned, Humanity of Christ in glory, in eternity. We stress the Humanity too exclusively at Christmas, and the Deity too exclusively after the Resurrection; almost as if Christ once became a man and then presently reverted to being simply God. We think of the Resurrection and Ascension (rightly) as great acts of God; less often as the triumph of Man."

Studying the Name

1. How did Jesus fulfill Daniel's vision of "one like a son of man"?

3. Why do you think Jesus cautioned his disciples against telling anyone that he was the Messiah?

4. Describe your image of the ideal father. How does this compare with your image of who God is?

5. Describe your image of the ideal son or daughter. How does this compare with your image of yourself in relationship to God?

6. How does Jesus as the ideal Human Being reflect your understanding of God's purpose for all human beings?

Passages for Continued Study

Deuteronomy 33:27; Daniel 7:13–14;
Matthew 12:38–42; 16:24–26; 20:20–28; 25:31–33; 26:63–66; 27:41–54;
Mark 9:2–7; John 3:16–17; 14:12–14; Romans 8:14–17, 28–30; 2 Corinthians 6:18;
Galatians 4:4–7; Hebrews 1:1–5; 1 John 3:1–4; 4:9–12; Revelation 1:12–18

49

GOOD SHEPHERD

ποιμὴν καλός

and Jesus' watchful, protecting care. It evokes a sense of belonging, intimacy, and trust, revealing the Good Shepherd as the one who lays down his life for his sheep. When you pray to the Good Shepherd, you are admitting your need for his care and your confidence in his ability to watch over and protect you.

Key Scripture
I am the good shepherd. The good shepherd lays down his life for the sheep.
(John 10:11)

Christ Reveals His Name in Scripture

"Very truly I tell you Pharisees, anyone who does not enter the sheep pen by the gate, but climbs in by some other way, is a thief and a robber. The one who enters by the gate is the shepherd of his sheep. The gatekeeper opens the gate for him, and the sheep listen to his voice. He calls his own sheep by name and leads them out. When he has brought out all his own, he goes on ahead of them, and his sheep follow him because they know his voice. But they will never follow a stranger; in fact, they will run away from him because they do not recognize a stranger's voice." Jesus used this figure of speech, but the Pharisees did not understand what he was telling them.

Therefore Jesus said again, "Very truly I tell you, I am the gate for the sheep. All who have come before me were thieves and robbers, but the sheep have not listened to them. I am the gate; whoever enters through me will be saved. They will come in and go out, and find pasture. The thief comes only to steal and kill and destroy; I have come that they may have life, and have it to the full.

"I am the good shepherd. The good shepherd lays down his life for the sheep. The hired hand is not the shepherd and does not own the sheep. So when he sees the wolf coming, he abandons the sheep and runs away. Then the wolf attacks the flock and scatters it. The man runs away because he is a hired hand and cares nothing for the sheep.

"I am the good shepherd; I know my sheep and my sheep know me — just as the Father knows me and I know the Father — and I lay down my life for the sheep. I have other sheep that are not of this sheep pen. I must bring them also. They too will listen to my voice, and there shall be one flock and one shepherd. The reason my Father loves me is that I lay down my life — only to take it up again. No one takes it from me, but I lay it down of my own accord. I have authority to lay it down and authority to take it up again. This command I received from my Father." (John 10:1 – 18)

Understanding the Name

Scripture uses various metaphors to describe God's people — a temple, a body, a bride, a garden, a vineyard, or a flock of sheep. Shepherding, in fact, was an important occupation in ancient Palestine. The role of the shepherd was to provide three things for the flock in his care: food, protection, and guidance.

Just as God's people are sometimes described in Scripture as a faithless bride, they are also pictured as a scattered flock. At such times, their leaders are portrayed as false shepherds who care little for the well-being of the flock entrusted to them. Without a shepherd to watch over them, the sheep scatter, becoming easy prey for wild animals and thieves.

Out of love for his wayward people, God promises to become their

Jesus shows us the lengths to which he as the Good Shepherd, or *Poimen Kalos* (poi-MAIN ka-LOS), will go in order to protect his sheep. Unlike those who merely work for pay, Jesus will never abandon his sheep. Instead, he will defend them with his own life. After his resurrection, Jesus exhorted Peter to follow his example by feeding his sheep. Leaders of the early church were referred to as "pastor," another translation of the Greek word *poimen*.

Studying the Name

1. Why do you think Jesus describes his relationship to his people as that of Shepherd and sheep?

2. This passage from John 10 contains both frightening and comforting images. It is frightening to think that thieves, robbers, and wolves want to prey on the sheep, but comforting to know that Jesus will go to any lengths to protect them. How do these images express spiritual realities?

3. The phrase "good shepherd" implies that there are also bad shepherds. How is it possible to tell the difference?

4. Describe an experience in which you recognized the voice of Jesus in your own life.

5. Describe ways in which Jesus has watched over and protected you as your Shepherd, even when you have walked through the valley of the shadow of death.

6. Who in your life is like a lost sheep whom God is seeking? What can you do to help bring this person into his flock?

50

SERVANT, SERVANT OF GOD, MAN OF SORROWS

EBED   *PAIS TOU THEOU*

ISH MAKOBOTH

Like most of us, Jesus' disciples were sometimes caught up with a sense of their own self-importance, at times even arguing with each other about which of them was greatest. Jesus startled them by reversing the natural order in which it is the weak who serve the strong. He assured them, instead, that he came not in order to control and dominate but in order to serve.

Though prophets, judges, and kings were called servants of God in the Bible, Jesus is the greatest of all God's servants, the Man of Sorrows who laid down his life in obedience to his Father. He is the Servant who through his suffering has saved us. When you pray to Jesus as Servant or as the Man of Sorrows, you are praying to the Lord who has loved you in the most passionate way possible, allowing himself to be nailed to a cross in order that you might have life and have it to the full.

Key Scriptures

He was despised and rejected, a man of sorrows, acquainted with bitterest grief.
(Isaiah 53:3 NLT)

The Son of Man did not come to be served, but to serve.
(Matthew 20:28)

Christ Reveals His Name in Scripture

See, my servant will prosper; he will be highly exalted....

My servant grew up in the Lord's presence like a tender green shoot, sprouting from a root in dry and sterile ground. There was nothing beautiful or majestic about his appearance, nothing to attract us to him. He was despised and rejected — a man of sorrows, acquainted with bitterest grief. We turned our backs on him and looked the other

and whoever wants to be first must be your slave — just as the Son of Man did not come to be served, but to serve, and to give his life as a ransom for many. (Matthew 20:26 – 28)

Understanding the Name

After God led the Israelites out of their slavery in Egypt, he did not treat them as slaves but as his own people, his sons and daughters. Though slavery was practiced in Israel, the Law forbade the forcible enslavement of freeborn individuals. To kidnap or sell such a person was to incur the death penalty. However, people could sell themselves in order to pay off their debts. Even so, Hebrew slaves were to be released after a certain number of years because no child of God was meant to live in perpetual bondage.

Though the Israelites were not considered God's slaves, they were considered his servants, freely putting his interests before their own, confident of his care and protection. To be God's servant involved living with an attitude of dependence and obedience. Scripture speaks of Moses, Joshua, Hannah, David, Isaiah, Mary the mother of Jesus, and many others as God's servants because they lived a life of faithful obedience.

The Servant Songs in Isaiah (42:1 – 4; 49:1 – 7; 50:4 – 9; 52:13 – 53:12) all speak of a mysterious Servant who would bring justice to the nations. Through his suffering this Man of Sorrows (ISH ma-ko-BOTH) would redeem many. The Jews may have understood this as a reference to Israel while early Christians understood these passages as messianic prophecies pointing to the suffering, death, and resurrection of Jesus Christ. By becoming one of us, Jesus suffered both with and for us. He was the Servant (E-bed) par excellence, the Servant of God (PICE tou the-OU), who not only obeyed God but obeyed to the point of death.

As his people, we are to follow his example, remembering his words that "whoever wants to become great among you must be your servant." Jesus' words make particular sense in light of the fact that in ancient times, a servant's status was directly related to the status of his master. To be a servant of the King of kings, then, is the greatest of privileges. It is no surprise to discover that the word "minister," derived from a Latin word, and the word "deacon," derived from a Greek word, both mean "servant."

Studying the Name

1. Describe an experience in which someone served you? How did it affect you?

3. How does the passage from Isaiah fit or fail to fit with your image of Jesus?

4. The Man of Sorrows was unattractive, despised, and rejected. Imagine Jesus just prior to his death. See in his face sorrow and bitter grief for the world. What drove him to endure such suffering?

5. When you think of Jesus' suffering, how does it make you feel about him, about yourself, about others?

6. To be God's servant involves living with an attitude of humble dependence and obedience. How can this attitude be expressed in you?

Passages for Continued Study

Psalm 34:22; Isaiah 42:1–4; 49:1–6; 50:4–9; 52:13–53:12; Matthew 11:28–30; 12:9–21; 24:42–51; John 13:1–5, 12–17; 1 Corinthians 9:19–23; Philippians 2:3–11; Revelation 22:1–5

51

THE REDEEMER

גָּאַל

LYTRON

Without a Redeemer willing and able to pay the high price necessary to liberate us from the power of sin, the story of our lives in this world would be nothing but a story of hopelessness. But because of Christ's redemptive love, we look forward with hope to a day when the world itself will be completely liberated from the power of sin and death. Until then we can express our faith in Christ by echoing the words of Scripture: "I know that my Redeemer lives and that in the end he will stand upon the earth. And ... in my flesh I will see God" (Job 19:25–26).

Key Scripture

For even the Son of Man did not come to be served, but to serve, and to give his life as a ransom for many. (Mark 10:45)

Christ Reveals His Name in Scripture

No one can redeem the life of another
   or give to God a sufficient ransom —
the ransom for a life is costly,
   no payment is ever enough —
so that someone should live on forever
   and not see decay. (Psalm 49:7 – 9)

Jesus called them together and said … "The Son of Man did not come to be served, but to serve, and to give his life as a ransom for many." (Mark 10:42, 45)

You are worthy to take the scroll and to open its seals, because you were slain, and with your blood you purchased for God members of every tribe and language and people and nation. (Revelation 5:9)

Understanding the Name

Redemption involves winning back, buying back, or repurchasing something that belongs to you or to someone else. The most dramatic example of this in the Old Testament was the exodus of God's people from Egypt. The former slaves praised *Yahweh* for acting as their Redeemer (Exodus 15:13). Subsequently, the prophets often linked redemption with freedom from political oppression.

But redemption also came into play within Israel itself because land, firstborn males, slaves, and people, objects, and animals consecrated to God all had to be redeemed by means of some kind of payment. In certain instances, such as when land had been sold to pay a debt (Leviticus 25:25 – 28) or a person had sold himself into slavery, the person's closest relative, called the "kinsman redeemer," had the right to step in and pay off the debt so that the land could be returned or the person could be freed.

God is often called "Redeemer" (*Ga'al*; ga-AL) in the Old Testament. Though the New Testament never directly refers to Jesus as the Redeemer, it makes clear that he offered himself as a ransom or as redemption (*Lytron*; LU-tron) when he died on the cross. Rather than liberating his people from political oppression, as many expected the Messiah to do, Jesus came to free his people from the demonic powers to which sin had enslaved them. His blood was the purchase price, offered not to Satan but to the Father as the ultimate expression of his love. By giving his life for them and for us, Jesus didn't make light of our guilt but lifted us, as one commentator has said, "out of disobedience into his own obedience," thereby freeing us from the bondage of sin and remaking us in his image.

Studying the Name

1. Why is Jesus worthy of purchasing each of us for God?

2. If Christ has purchased you with his blood, what are the implications for your sense of self-worth? For your sense of the worth of others?

3. The passage from Revelation indicates that you were purchased *for* God. If that is so, what are the implications for your life?

4. Christ did not only free you from the slavery of sin, he also secured for you eternal life where you will be completely free from the ravages of sin, sickness, suffering, and sorrow. What do you look forward to seeing eradicated from your life? What do you envision attaining?

5. Scripture says that Jesus has purchased members from every tribe and language and people and nation. How diverse is your denomination or local church? Are you happy with the status quo? Why or why not?

Passages for Continued Study

Exodus 12:12; Deuteronomy 7:8; 2 Samuel 7:22; Job 19:25–26; Psalms 49:15; 130:7–8; Isaiah 41:14; 54:5; Jeremiah 50:33–34; Luke 1:67–75; 21:25–28; Romans 8:22–25; Ephesians 1:3–10; Revelation 5:6–9

52

I Am

ἐγώ εἰμι

Ego Eimi

In Jesus we have the richest, most vivid picture of God imaginable. No longer does God seem implacably remote, displeased with the world he has made. Instead, he bends toward us, sharing our weakness and shouldering our burdens. Through the perfect offering of his life he becomes our Way back to the Father. He is the true Vine in which we abide, bearing fruit for God's kingdom. He is the loving God who will never abandon us, but who will be present with us always, leading us to life eternal.

Key Scriptures

Moses said to God, "Suppose I go to the Israelites and say to them, 'The God of your fathers has sent me to you,' and they ask me, 'What is his name?' Then what shall I tell them?"God said to Moses, "I AM WHO I AM. You are to say to the Israelites: 'I AM has sent me to you.'" (Exodus 3:13–14)

"You are not yet fifty years old," the Jews said to him [Jesus], "and you have seen Abraham!""I tell you the truth," Jesus answered, "before Abraham was born, I am!" (John 8:57–58)

Christ Reveals His Name in Scripture

Moses said to God, "Suppose I go to the Israelites and say to them, 'The God of your fathers has sent me to you,' and they ask me, 'What is his name?' Then what shall I tell them?"

God said to Moses, "I am who I am. This is what you are to say to the Israelites: 'I am has sent me to you.'" (Exodus 3:13–14)

"I ⁓⁓⁓ ⁓⁓⁓⁓⁓ glory for myself; but there is one who seeks it,

Jesus replied, "If I glorify myself, my glory means nothing. My Father, whom you claim as your God, is the one who glorifies me. Though you do not know him, I know him. If I said I did not, I would be a liar like you, but I do know him and obey his word. Your father Abraham rejoiced at the thought of seeing my day; he saw it and was glad."

"You are not yet fifty years old," the Jews said to him, "and you have seen Abraham!"

"Very truly I tell you," Jesus answered, "before Abraham was born, I am!" At this, they picked up stones to stone him, but Jesus hid himself, slipping away from the temple grounds. (John 8:50–59)

Understanding the Name

When Moses first encountered God in the wilderness in the figure of a burning bush, he asked God to reveal his name. But the reply he received seemed only to add to the mystery of who God is. Instead of describing himself as the Living God or the Almighty God or the Everlasting God or the Creator God, the Lord instructed Moses, saying, "This is what you are to say to the Israelites: 'I AM has sent me to you.'" In fact, the name "I AM" closely related to the four Hebrew consonants that make up the name *Yahweh*, the covenant name of God in the Old Testament. Though the exact meaning of this name is difficult to know with certainty, the Lord may have been revealing himself not only as the God who has always existed but also as the God who is always present with his people.

When Jesus was being attacked by the religious leaders who failed to recognize him as the Messiah, he shocked them not by claiming to be the Messiah but by identifying himself with *Yahweh*, saying: "Before Abraham was born, *I am*." Recognizing that Jesus was claiming to be divine, the scandalized religious leaders tried to stone him. In fact, John's gospel contains several self-descriptions of Jesus introduced by the emphatic expression *Ego Eimi* (e-GO ay-MEE), "I am."

I am the bread of life. (6:35)
I am the light of the world. (8:12)
Before Abraham was born, I am. (8:58)
I am the gate for the sheep. (10:7)
I am the good shepherd. (10:11)
I am the resurrection and the life. (11:25)
I am the way and the truth and the life. (14:6)
I am the true vine, and my Father is the gardener. (15:1)

Jesus emphatically described himself as the "resurrection and the life," "the way and the truth and the life," and the "true vine." Each of these images has something important to reveal to us about the character and purpose of Jesus Christ.

Studying the Name

1. Some scholars think that by saying "I AM WHO I AM," God was saying he would always be present with his people. How have you experienced God's faithful presence in your life?

3. Why do you think the religious leaders responded to the "good news" as though it were "bad news"?

4. Jesus' response to his disciples' fear could literally be translated: "Take courage! I am." How might your knowledge of Jesus' presence help you to take courage in fearful times?

5. Before his crucifixion, Jesus revealed himself to his disciples, saying, "I am the way and the truth and the life." What is Jesus the way to?

6. In John 15:1–5 Jesus speaks of himself as the true vine and calls us to remain in him. What does it mean to "remain in the vine"? Think about your hardships in the light of "pruning."

Passages for Continued Study

Matthew 16:15–16; 28:20; Mark 14:25–27, 61–62;
John 11:21–26; 14:1–6; 15:1–16; 18:4–6; Revelation 1:8; 17; 21:6

SELECTED BIBLIOGRAPHY

Arthur, Kay. *Lord, I Want to Know You*. Colorado Springs, CO: Waterbrook, 1992, 2000.

Barker, Kenneth L., and John Kohlenberger III, eds. *Zondervan NIV Bible Commentary*. 2 vols. Grand Rapids: Zondervan, 1994.

bleday, 1992.

Hemphill, Ken. *The Names of God*. Nashville: Broadman & Holman, 2001.

Kittel, Gerhard, and Gerhard Friedrich, eds. *Theological Dictionary of the New Testament: Abridged in One Volume*. Translated and abridged by Geoffrey W. Bomiley. Grand Rapids: Eerdmans, 1985.

Lockyer, Herbert. *All the Divine Names and Titles in the Bible*. Grand Rapids: Zondervan, 1975.

Rhodes, Tricia McCary. *At the Name of Jesus*. Minneapolis: Bethany, 2003.

Richards, Lawrence O. *Every Name of God in the Bible*. Nashville: Thomas Nelson, 2001.

———. *New International Encyclopedia of Bible Words*. Grand Rapids: Zondervan, 1999.

Shelly, Rubel. *The Names of Jesus*. West Monroe, LA: Howard, 1999.

Simpson, A. B. *The Names of Jesus*. Harrisburg, PA: Christian Publications, 1967.

Stone, Nathan. *Names of God*. Chicago: Moody Press, 1944.

Tenney, Merrill C., ed. *Zondervan Pictorial Encyclopedia of the Bible*. 5 vols. Grand Rapids: Zondervan, 1975, 1976.

Towns, Elmer L. *My Father's Names*. Ventura, CA: Regal, 1991.

———. *The Names of Jesus*. Colorado Springs, CO: Accent, 1987.

VanGemeren, Willem A. *New International Dictionary of Old Testament Theology and Exegesis*. 5 vols. Grand Rapids: Zondervan, 1997.

Watley, William D. *Exalting the Names of Jesus*. Valley Forge, PA: Judson, 2002.

Wiersbe, Warren W., ed. *Classic Sermons on the Names of God*. Grand Rapids: Kregel, 1993.

———. *The Wonderful Names of Jesus*. Lincoln, NE: Back to the Bible, 1980.